THE DUKE'S MAYONNAISE
COOKBOOK

FAMILY RECIPE
SINCE 1917

Duke's

REAL
MAYONNAISE

SMOOTH & CREAMY

75 Recipes Celebrating the Perfect Condiment

ASHLEY STRICKLAND FREEMAN

FOREWORD BY NATHALIE DUPREE, AUTHOR OF *MASTERING THE ART OF SOUTHERN COOKING*

PHOTOGRAPHY BY MARY BRITTON SENSENEY
ILLUSTRATIONS BY EMILY WALLACE

GRAND CENTRAL
PUBLISHING

NEW YORK   BOSTON

Grand Central Publishing
Hachette Book Group
1290 Avenue of the Americas, New York, NY 10104
grandcentralpublishing.com
twitter.com/grandcentralpub

First Edition: June 2020

Grand Central Publishing is a division of Hachette Book Group, Inc. The Grand Central
Publishing name and logo is a trademark of Hachette Book Group, Inc.

The publisher is not responsible for websites (or their content)
that are not owned by the publisher.

The Hachette Speakers Bureau provides a wide range of authors for speaking events.
To find out more, go to www.hachettespeakersbureau.com or call (866) 376-6591.

Print book interior design by Laura Palese

Library of Congress Control Number: 2020930115
ISBNs: 978-1-5387-1734-9 (hardcover); 978-1-5387-1735-6 (ebook)

Printed in the United States of America

WOR

10 9 8 7 6 5 4 3 2 1

TO

Mom & Dad,

who taught me the love
of cooking, the love of meals
with family, and, of course,
the love of Duke's.

Foreword

BY NATHALIE DUPREE

When Ashley told me she was writing this book about Duke's Mayonnaise, and using some of her favorite recipes from all the travels she and her family have taken, I wasn't surprised. She's always touted Duke's and talked about how it's often her secret ingredient in her recipes.

Of course, I'm a Duke's lover, too, like anyone who grew up in the South. In fact, as you'll see from the many quotes from the chefs that are included throughout this book, most of us don't think of Duke's as just mayonnaise; we think of it as a unique spread that can enhance any sandwich—either by itself with just a bit of bacon, or as part of a recipe, as in Ashley's mother's Pimento Cheese, the Basil Mayo for her Avocado BLTs, or the Grilled Okra with Tomato Aïoli. Duke's is also the not-so-secret-anymore ingredient in cakes that makes them moist; it's the key ingredient for Ashley's Ice Cream Cookie Sandwiches that makes the cookies soft and tender; and when used as a marinade, it adds flavor and tenderizes the meat at the same time. Many Southern chefs and cooks—me included—have promoted Duke's just because we love it and feel like it's an essential ingredient in a recipe. I even did a free TV spot for it once along with some other cooks.

Ashley's beloved grandmother was a close friend of my former mother-in-law, who I loved dearly as well. After graduating from college and culinary school, Ashley tested and developed recipes for my books and then went on to work for Oxmoor House, doing what she does best: creating recipes and writing cookbooks. Her talent shines through in this book and these recipes. Keep looking and cooking. Ashley has good fixings for you and your family.

A NOTE FROM DUKE'S

When Eugenia Thomas Duke created Duke's Mayonnaise back in 1917, I don't think she would've ever imagined that 103 years later, an entire cookbook would be crafted in honor of her humble mixture of eggs and oil. It's of no surprise to us, of course, since we enjoy it daily in so many ways and have always considered it to be the secret to great food.

Duke's has gone from a South Carolina staple to being sold in 42 states in the Union, raising the bar for mayonnaise all across the country and delighting transplanted southerners far from home. We are excited to introduce new consumers to the smooth and creamy, tangy goodness that is Duke's, and eager to offer them new and different ways to enjoy it.

So when Ashley first approached us about writing a cookbook celebrating her favorite condiment, we said "Bring it on!" Inspired by the success that others have had using Duke's to make chocolate cake, scrambled eggs, and grilled cheese, Ashley has been cooking and baking up a storm to see what else can be improved using a dollop of Duke's. Her delicious creations have been perfected in her home kitchen and taste-tested by her luckiest friends in Charleston and Savannah. (Her banana bread is to die for!) Ashley has talked with countless chefs and home cooks who consider a jar of Duke's a must-have, not only in their home kitchens, but in their restaurants as well.

We hope Ashley's book becomes a well-used addition to your esteemed cookbook library. The spirit of Eugenia lives on in all those who share delicious homemade food with their family and friends.

—WITH LOVE FROM DUKE'S, SAUER BRANDS, INC.

Introduction

Food is my love language. I think my parents knew pretty early on that I was going to be a cookbook writer, or at least have a career in food. For fun I would read my mom's *Christmas with Southern Living* cookbooks and make peanut-butter-and-jelly on Ritz cracker "hors d'oeuvres." When most kids wrote letters home from summer camp about friends they were making or the hike they'd gone on, I wrote about what we ate for each meal at the dining hall. And nothing changed as I got older. When we are eating lunch, I'm planning dinner in my head. I'm almost never not thinking about food, so to have this cookbook filled with my recipes is a dream come true. So many of my fondest memories involve food—sitting around a table with family or friends, sharing something I've created, or experiencing a local dish in a foreign country.

While my love language is food, travel is my passion. My grandmother was undersecretary of the Treasury for President Jimmy Carter and therefore traveled all over the world. After her tenure for his administration, she served on several boards that allowed her and my family to travel. So the travel bug bit me early and with fervor. One of Mimi's (my grandmother's) claims to fame was chasing after Michelin stars: If we were ever within a couple hundred miles of a Michelin-starred restaurant, we would spend the day traveling to eat there. Possibly much to my family's chagrin, this is how I plan our trips today: around food. I've been fortunate to explore a lot of the United States, Europe, and eventually Asia with my husband, and what I loved most about those trips was seeing how people different from me combine flavors in their local cuisine.

Food is transformative—a smell or taste can quickly take you back to somewhere you had been long ago. When I am asked about a particular place, it's not uncommon for me to remember it because of a food experience. In Rome, that's where I had the most amazing crespelles, covered in a creamy cheese sauce and baked up until bubbly brown. It took us three hours of getting lost to find the trattoria serving them, but it was worth it. Or in Shenzhen, China, when my husband, Chris, and I were looking for the gigantic shopping mall where we could have clothes custom made, and we took a wrong turn. We ended up in a different neighborhood and happened upon a soup dumpling shop. The menu was only in Chinese, so we resorted to pointing to the table next to us and their dumplings to convey what we wanted. To this day, I have never had a better dumpling. Or in Koloa Town, Kauai, where our first stop after my mother-in-law picks us up from the airport is always the Fish Market to get the ahi poke bowl—a heavenly blend of fresh tuna, sesame oil, seaweed flakes, eel sauce, and spicy mayo. And even memories of when I was young—the strawberry shortcake my Uncle Brooks and Aunt Vilma would bring to our Beasley family reunions in Stilson, Georgia. After sliding down the sliding board (on a towel so we wouldn't burn our fannies) dozens of times, we would join what seemed like hundreds of extended family members in the school cafeteria and load our plates down with every type of field pea imaginable, fried chicken, pineapple sandwiches, tomato sandwiches, and casseroles galore, wash it all down with sweet tea, and round out the meal with a hunk of strawberry shortcake.

Not all of my food memories are pleasant, however. What comes to mind in particular was when Chris and I were staying at the marine station in Kaohsiung, Taiwan. The station was in a beautiful but remote location, and we didn't have a car or any way to get around. We thought we were all set with the groceries we had brought, but when the staff left on Friday afternoon for the weekend, we soon realized that was not the case. There was no way to cook our food. No hot pot, microwave, nothing. So, to "cook" our spaghetti noodles, we let them bathe in hot water (from one of those drink dispensers—you know the ones that you use to make hot tea). An hour later, we had soggy, crunchy spaghetti with room-temperature sauce right from the jar. That was probably the worst meal I've ever had.

The places I've visited often serve as inspiration for many of the recipes I create. So, when tasked with coming up with an idea for a cookbook, I knew I wanted to share flavors from my travels as well as special recipes from my childhood. What better ingredient to tie those two together than Duke's?

I grew up on Duke's Mayonnaise. If you were to open my mother's pantry door this afternoon, you'd see her upcycled, yellow-topped Duke's Mayonnaise jars filled with all-purpose flour, cornmeal, and powdered sugar lining the shelves. Duke's is my mom's secret ingredient in her famous pimento cheese, is the perfect creamy condiment to slather on the tomato sandwiches we brought to those family reunions each May, and contributes the ideal tanginess to make my deviled eggs a must-have at any get-together. I wouldn't dream of buying any other mayo, and I'm not the only one. Duke's has a cult following and is celebrated in this book with testimonials from some of my favorite chefs and authors scattered throughout the recipes.

Now that I'm a grown-up (and a recipe developer and food stylist by trade), I've upcycled not just mayo jars, but also my recipes to include Duke's Mayonnaise. Think of what mayonnaise actually is: a beautiful emulsification of eggs and oil and a touch of vinegar for acidity, all ingredients vital to cooking and baking. So, what's my secret to the flakiest pie crust? It's Duke's. Want to know how to make *the* fluffiest scrambled eggs? Duke's. How to make grilled cheese even better? Duke's again. A way to create a tender crumb in a cake or doughnut? You guessed it. Sure, Duke's is essential in everyday favorites like deviled eggs and chicken salad, but it's also the unexpected secret ingredient to making everything from Overnight Churro Waffles to Corn and Basil Hush Puppies into home run recipes.

From breakfast to dessert, Duke's is my secret ingredient for amazing recipes, and it's the ingredient that's been missing from yours. *The Duke's Mayonnaise Cookbook* is a compilation of recipes inspired by my travels across the country and around the world. Whether in classic favorites like Green Tomato Pie or unexpected dishes like Miso-Glazed Salmon and Sticky Toffee Puddings, you'll discover how versatile Duke's Mayonnaise really is.

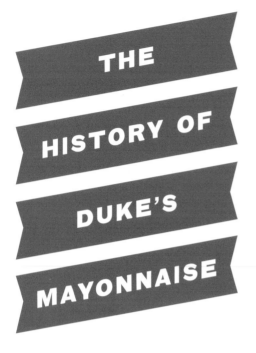

THE HISTORY OF DUKE'S MAYONNAISE

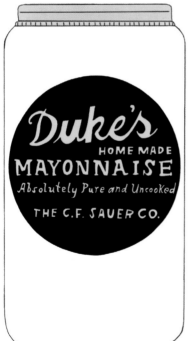

Duke's
HOME MADE
MAYONNAISE
Absolutely Pure and Uncooked
THE C.F. SAUER CO.

After over one hundred years, the Duke's recipe remains the same as it was in 1917 when Eugenia Duke created it in her kitchen in Greenville, South Carolina. At the time, she didn't realize the gold mine she was sitting on, but instead focused on the sandwiches she made using her homemade mayonnaise. Over the years her business sense allowed her to be a pioneer in the industry, and we have her to thank for the deliciousness that is Duke's.

Eugenia Thomas was born in Columbus, Georgia, the youngest of ten children. At 19 years old, she married Henry Duke, and about ten years later, she, Henry, and daughter Martha moved to Greenville, South Carolina, for his job at the Southern Power Company.

Greenville's economy prospered because of a booming textile industry and laid a firm foundation for Eugenia and what would become her business. In 1917, after the United States joined the Allies in World War I, Greenville witnessed an influx of soldiers who came to train at nearby Camp Sevier, a National Guard training camp. Recognizing business potential, Eugenia Duke began selling sandwiches featuring her homemade mayonnaise to the hungry soldiers, and her success continued. After selling her 11,000th sandwich, she purchased a delivery truck to help distribute the sandwiches that were in such high demand. The sandwiches were so popular that years later, after the war, soldiers would write to Eugenia requesting that she share her sandwich recipes and send jars of her homemade mayonnaise. Locals were also fans of Eugenia's sandwiches and began asking if they too could purchase them. So she began selling her sandwiches at local drugstores and then converted the first floor of the Ottaray Hotel into Duke's Tea Room.

By the beginning of 1920, Eugenia was running out of room in her home kitchen to keep up with all of the sandwich orders coming in, so she built a separate kitchen on her property. In 1923, C.B. Boyd, Eugenia's best salesman, made an important observation: While the sandwiches were in fact delicious, it was the unique homemade mayonnaise used on the sandwiches that made everyone come back for more. Boyd convinced Eugenia to focus more on her mayonnaise; as a result, she began jarring the spread and selling it as a separate product. Along with her accountant, J. Allen Hart, Eugenia opened an office on South Main Street in Greenville and began producing what we now enjoy as Duke's Mayonnaise in an old carriage factory building. Not surprisingly, sales for the mayonnaise soared, so she sold the sandwich company to Hart and focused her attention on the mayonnaise business.

In 1929, after struggling to keep up with the ever-expanding business, Eugenia sold the business to the C.F. Sauer Company based out of Richmond, Virginia. She served as the spokeswoman for Duke's but eventually moved out West to be closer to her daughter.

The C.F. Sauer Company continued to grow the business and expand the reach of Duke's Mayonnaise all over the Southeast. In the 1940s, *The Joan Brooks Show,* a TV variety show that featured popular actors and musicians, was sponsored solely by Sauer. Hollace Shaw, a famous actress at the time, became one of the faces of "The House of Sauer" advertisements that played during the commercial breaks and helped expand the popularity of the product.

Sauer continued to grow the business and adapted to changing trends, introducing light mayonnaise in the 1980s, being the first in innovating a squeeze bottle in 2003, and switching from glass jars to plastic in 2006. In June 2019, the C.F. Sauer Company sold the food business to Charlotte, North Carolina–based equity firm Falfurrias Capital Partners, who promise to keep the tradition alive. For this, we Duke's fans are thankful.

Many will say Duke's has a cult following, and it's easy to see why. The unique sugar-free recipe makes it an extremely versatile ingredient and has garnered a loyal and fervent fan base—from well-known chefs to home cooks. Why make mayonnaise from scratch when the perfect condiment already exists? Restaurants proudly proclaim their use of Duke's Mayonnaise on their menus; the condiment has inspired art, from illustrations and paintings to jewelry; and some folks have gone as far as having an image of Duke's jar tattooed on their body. Today, Duke's can be found in over forty states—a sure sign that the word is getting out.

How to Use This Book

The recipes in this book are geared toward home cooks. I started my career in a test kitchen creating recipes for cookbooks, and I develop the same types of recipes today. You don't need a fancy kitchen for the recipes here. If I call for a special pan, I also offer alternatives. The book is divided into chapters for Breakfast and Brunch, Lunch (Salads, Soups, and Sandwiches), Dinner (Main Dishes), Snacks and Sides, and Desserts. Generally, each chapter begins with the easiest recipes first and progresses into the more advanced recipes. If you are a beginner cook, I recommend working your way through each chapter from easiest to hardest. Where I can, I've provided tips to help. Below you'll also find helpful information on how to get the best results from the recipes in this book.

General Recipe Guidelines

- While other types of Duke's Mayonnaise (light, olive oil, and heavy-duty) may work in these recipes, I tested with regular Duke's.

- Be sure to use dry measuring cups for things like mayonnaise, flour, and sugar and liquid measuring cups for things like milk, broth, and water.

- When measuring dry ingredients like flour and powdered sugar that can "pack" down, spoon the ingredient into the dry measuring cup and level with a knife as opposed to scooping the measuring cup into the ingredient.

- I tested and developed the recipes using a standard electric oven and standard electric stovetop. Be aware that if you use a convection oven, your bake times will be different.

- When recipes call for you to "grease and flour" a pan, I use a little vegetable shortening and spread it on with a paper towel. Then, I sprinkle in some flour and shake it around to fully coat the pan. A final "bang" of the pan, and the excess flour shakes off.

- Unless otherwise stated, I tested with regular table salt and freshly ground black pepper for "salt and pepper."

If you were to make every single recipe in this book, here are the pans and equipment you would need:

Baking pans: 8-inch round and 9-inch round cake pans; 9- x 5-inch loaf pan; 8-inch square pan; Bundt pan; 12-well muffin tin; rimmed baking sheet; mini Bundt pan (you can also use a muffin tin here); 2-quart baking pan; 13- x 9-inch baking pan; ramekins; pie plate; 10-inch tart pan; mini fluted egg tart molds (again, you can also use a muffin tin)

Saucepans and skillets: large nonstick skillet; Dutch oven or heavy stockpot; small and medium saucepans; cast-iron skillet

Appliances: waffle iron; heavy stand mixer; food processor; immersion or stand blender; outdoor grill (or you can use a grill pan); pasta roller (or follow the rolling pin instructions)

Other tools: dry and liquid measuring cups; measuring spoons; cookie scoop (helpful but not necessary); doughnut cutter (or round cookie or biscuit cutters); candy thermometer; instant-read thermometer; tongs; colander; metal or wooden skewers; cooling rack; rolling pin; grill basket (or follow the alternative option)

CHAPTER ONE

BREAKFAST
and
BRUNCH

SECRET-INGREDIENT
Scrambled Eggs 4

Breakfast Strata 15

PIMENTO CHEESE GRITS 8

CHORIZO HASH
WITH SPICY SMOKED PAPRIKA SAUCE 5

BLUEBERRY STREUSEL MUFFINS 13

AVOCADO TOAST
WITH SMOKED SALMON AND SOFT-BOILED EGGS 16

CINNAMON ROLLS
with Cream Cheese Glaze 38

Easy Buttermilk Biscuits 21

Old-Fashioned Doughnuts with Mixed Berry Glaze 42

OVERNIGHT CHURRO WAFFLES 19

HAM, MUSHROOM, AND COMTÉ OMELETS 22

SUN-DRIED TOMATO, GOAT CHEESE, AND SPINACH QUICHE 29

BANANAS FOSTER BREAD WITH BROWNED BUTTER-RUM GLAZE 26

EARL GREY SCONES 32

PEACHES AND CREAM CRÊPES 35

Secret-Ingredient

Scrambled Eggs

MAKES 4 SERVINGS

I learned this trick from Alton Brown: Whisk a little mayonnaise into eggs before scrambling them, and they'll come out super creamy and fluffy. So, I tried it and am a believer. For a heartier dish, scramble the eggs, then fold in your favorite add-ins, such as shredded Cheddar cheese, crumbled bacon, or sautéed vegetables.

8	large eggs
¼	cup Duke's Mayonnaise
¼	teaspoon salt
¼	teaspoon freshly ground pepper
2	tablespoons salted butter
2	tablespoons chopped fresh chives

1. Whisk together the eggs, mayonnaise, salt, and pepper in a medium bowl.

2. Melt the butter in a large nonstick skillet over medium-high heat. Add the egg mixture. Cook, stirring occasionally with a spatula to create large curds. Cook until the eggs are firm but still creamy. Sprinkle with the chives before serving.

Chorizo Hash

with SPICY SMOKED PAPRIKA SAUCE

MAKES 4 SERVINGS

~ ~ ~ ~ ~ ~ ~ ~ ~ ~ ~ ~ ~ ~ ~ ~ ~ ~ ~ ~

Patatas bravas is one of my favorite Spanish tapas dishes, and the most recent (and memorable) rendition I had was at Cúrate in Asheville, North Carolina, on an annual girls' trip with friends from high school. What's not to love about crispy skillet-fried chunks of potato topped with a spicy mayonnaise-based sauce? This breakfast version includes sausage and vegetables and is topped with a fried egg.

~ ~ ~ ~ ~ ~ ~ ~ ~ ~ ~ ~ ~ ~ ~ ~ ~ ~ ~ ~

	Spicy Smoked Paprika Sauce (recipe follows)
1	pound fresh chorizo sausage, casings removed (if applicable)
3	tablespoons vegetable oil, divided
1½	pounds baby Dutch Yellow potatoes, cut into bite-size pieces
1	red onion, cut into bite-size pieces
2	red bell peppers, cut into bite-size pieces
4	large eggs
	Salt and freshly ground pepper
	Fresh cilantro leaves

1. Make the Spicy Smoked Paprika Sauce. Set aside.

2. Heat a large skillet over medium-high heat. Add the chorizo and cook, stirring occasionally, for 5 to 6 minutes, until the chorizo is browned and crumbles. Remove from the skillet and keep warm.

3. Add 2 tablespoons of the oil to the skillet. Stir in the potatoes and onion, and reduce the heat to medium. Cover the skillet and cook for 5 minutes, stirring occasionally, until the potatoes begin to brown. Uncover and cook for 5 more minutes.

4. Add the peppers and cook for 3 minutes, until the vegetables are tender. Stir in the cooked chorizo.

Recipe Continues

5. Meanwhile, heat the remaining 1 tablespoon oil in a large nonstick skillet over medium-high heat. Add the eggs and cook for 1 to 2 minutes on each side, or to desired doneness.

6. Season the hash with salt and pepper to taste. Divide among serving plates or individual skillets. Top each serving with cilantro and a fried egg, and serve with the Spicy Smoked Paprika Sauce.

TASTY TIP

All chorizo sausages are not the same. In this recipe, I like to use fresh, uncooked chorizo.

You can also use fully cooked chorizo if you prefer. Just be sure not to buy the dry, cured chorizo that looks like pepperoni. The texture will be too tough for this hash.

Spicy SMOKED PAPRIKA SAUCE

Makes about ²/₃ cup

½ CUP DUKE'S MAYONNAISE

1 TABLESPOON HOT SAUCE

1 TABLESPOON SMOKED PAPRIKA

1 TEASPOON FRESH LIME JUICE

1 TEASPOON HONEY

Stir together all the ingredients in a small bowl. Refrigerate until ready to serve or up to 2 days.

SHOWN ON PAGE 10

Pimento Cheese Grits

MAKES 6 TO 8 SERVINGS

To me, grits are the perfect comfort food. When I was growing up, they were my mom's cure-all for everything from a cold or stomachache to a heartbreak. Another recipe that reminds me of my mom is pimento cheese, although her version is a little different from mine. When stirred into grits, pimento cheese provides the perfect blend of cheese and spices. You'll have some left over, so serve with celery sticks or your favorite cracker.

2	cups whole milk
2	cups water
1	teaspoon salt
1	cup stone-ground white or yellow grits
1	cup Pimento Cheese (recipe follows), plus more for serving if desired

1. Bring the milk, water, and salt to a boil in a medium saucepan. Slowly whisk in the grits.

2. Reduce the heat to low and simmer, uncovered, for 30 to 35 minutes, stirring frequently and adding more water if needed, to reach desired consistency.

3. While the grits cook, prepare the Pimento Cheese.

4. Stir the Pimento Cheese into the grits and simmer until the cheese is melted. Divide the grits evenly among serving bowls and top with additional Pimento Cheese, if desired.

Pimento CHEESE

Makes about 2 cups

1 (8-OUNCE) BLOCK EXTRA-SHARP CHEDDAR CHEESE, SHREDDED

4 OUNCES SHARP WHITE CHEDDAR CHEESE, SHREDDED

1 TABLESPOON GRATED ONION

1 (4-OUNCE) JAR DICED PIMENTOS, DRAINED

½ CUP DUKE'S MAYONNAISE

1 TABLESPOON WORCESTERSHIRE SAUCE

1 TEASPOON FRESH LEMON JUICE

¼ TEASPOON CAYENNE PEPPER

1. Combine the cheeses, onion, and pimentos in a medium bowl.

2. Stir together the mayonnaise, Worcestershire sauce, lemon juice, and cayenne pepper in a separate small bowl. Pour over the cheese mixture and stir well to combine. Refrigerate until ready to serve or up to 3 days.

TASTY TIP
Use a box grater or Microplane to grate the onion.

Pimento
Cheese Grits,
PAGE 8

Ham,
Mushroom,
and Comté
Omelets,
PAGE 22

Easy
Buttermilk
Biscuits,
PAGE 21

Blueberry Streusel Muffins

MAKES 1 DOZEN MUFFINS

I've always loved blueberry muffins, and these are my favorite. They also happen to be a favorite of my son's, and since they aren't too sweet I don't mind serving him one for breakfast. Duke's tenderizes the crumb and makes the muffins super moist. A zing from lemon zest and a sugary praline-inspired streusel topping make them heavenly.

	Streusel Topping (recipe follows)
2	cups all-purpose flour, divided
1½	cups fresh blueberries
1	tablespoon baking powder
1	cup whole milk
¼	cup vegetable oil
⅓	cup granulated sugar
3	tablespoons Duke's Mayonnaise
2	teaspoons grated lemon zest
1	large egg
1	teaspoon vanilla extract

TASTY TIP

You can also use frozen blueberries.

Just make sure they are fully thawed and dried before tossing them in the flour. Tossing the berries in flour helps to suspend them in the batter instead of sinking to the bottom of the muffin.

1. Preheat the oven to 400°F. Place paper liners in a 12-well muffin tin. Coat the liners with cooking spray.

2. Prepare the Streusel Topping and set aside.

3. Toss 1 tablespoon of the flour with the blueberries and set aside. Stir together the remaining flour and baking powder in a small bowl.

4. Whisk together the milk, oil, granulated sugar, mayonnaise, lemon zest, egg, and vanilla until combined. Add the flour mixture and stir until the batter is smooth. Add the blueberries and gently fold to combine.

5. Divide the batter evenly among the muffin liners and sprinkle with the Streusel Topping. Bake the muffins at 400°F for 20 to 23 minutes, until a toothpick inserted in the center comes out clean. Let the muffins cool in the pan for 5 minutes before removing from the tin to wire racks to cool.

Recipe Continues

Streusel TOPPING

Makes about 1¼ cups

½ CUP ALL-PURPOSE FLOUR

½ CUP CHOPPED PECANS

⅓ CUP FIRMLY PACKED BROWN SUGAR

½ TEASPOON GROUND CINNAMON

¼ CUP SALTED BUTTER, MELTED

Stir together all the ingredients. Use your fingers to press
the mixture into large clumps, if desired.

Breakfast Strata

MAKES 6 TO 8 SERVINGS

~~~~~~

This savory breakfast bread pudding reminds me of Christmas mornings growing up. We would always have a square of the cheesy casserole after opening presents, first at home and then again with my grandparents, Nany and Marguite, at their house. I didn't mind having it more than once—it's that good! It's a great make-ahead brunch dish—assemble it the night before and bake the morning of. Stale bread actually works best here to prevent sogginess. You could also toast fresher bread cubes or leave them on a baking sheet for about an hour to dry them out.

~~~~~~

1	**pound day-old crusty bread loaf (such as French or Italian bread), cubed**
1	**pound bulk pork breakfast sausage**
1	**(8-ounce) block sharp Cheddar cheese, shredded**
6	**large eggs**
2	**cups whole milk**
⅓	**cup Duke's Mayonnaise**
2	**teaspoons yellow mustard**
¼	**teaspoon salt**
¼	**teaspoon freshly ground pepper**

1. Lightly grease a 13- x 9-inch baking dish. Arrange the bread cubes in the baking dish.

2. Cook the sausage in a large skillet over medium-high heat for 5 to 6 minutes, until browned and crumbled. Add to the bread cubes along with the cheese, tossing to disperse evenly.

3. Whisk together the eggs, milk, mayonnaise, mustard, salt, and pepper. Pour over the bread mixture. Press down on the bread cubes to allow them to soak in the egg mixture. Cover and refrigerate overnight.

4. Preheat the oven to 350°F. Remove the casserole from the refrigerator and uncover. Bake the casserole, uncovered, for 35 to 40 minutes, until the top is browned and the center is set. Cut into squares to serve.

Avocado Toast

with

SMOKED SALMON AND SOFT-BOILED EGGS

MAKES 4 SERVINGS

4	large eggs
8	slices bakery bread
7	tablespoons Duke's Mayonnaise, divided
3	large avocados, divided
1	tablespoon chopped fresh dill
2	teaspoons fresh lemon juice
¼	teaspoon salt
¼	teaspoon freshly ground pepper
1	(4-ounce) package sliced smoked salmon
	Fresh dill sprigs (optional)

This breakfast toast combines two of my favorite things: creamy avocado and jammy soft-boiled eggs. Add salty smoked salmon and some fresh dill and you've got a wholesome breakfast to get your day started off right. I'm also a firm believer that bacon makes everything better, so serve with a few slices on the side to round out the meal. If you're not a fan of soft-boiled eggs, feel free to fry or hard-cook them to your liking.

1. Preheat the oven to 400°F. Bring a medium saucepan of water to a boil. Place a medium bowl of ice and water next to the saucepan. Gently add the eggs to the boiling water with a slotted spoon and boil for 6 minutes and 30 seconds. Drain the eggs and immediately plunge in the ice water.

2. Brush one side of the bread slices with 4 tablespoons of the mayonnaise and place in a single layer, mayonnaise side up, on a rimmed baking sheet. Bake at 400°F for 5 minutes, or until the bread is toasted.

3. Pit, peel, and chop 2 avocados and place in a medium bowl. Add the remaining 3 tablespoons mayonnaise, the dill, lemon juice, salt, and pepper. Mash the mixture with a fork to desired consistency. Pit, peel, and slice the remaining avocado.

4. To serve, spread the avocado mash evenly onto the toasts. Peel the eggs and cut each in half. Top the toasts with avocado slices, smoked salmon, and egg halves. Garnish with dill sprigs if desired.

Overnight Churro Waffles

MAKES 16 SILVER DOLLAR–SIZE WAFFLES

~ ~

These decadent churro-inspired waffles are sure to be a hit in your house. What I love best about them is that you can make the yeast batter the night before and have it ready to go the next morning. The sugary cinnamon topping makes these sweet enough to eat without syrup, but for the ultimate authentic churro experience serve with hot caramel or fudge if you'd like.

~ ~

1½	cups whole milk	¾	cup salted butter, melted, divided
2	tablespoons sugar	1½	teaspoons vanilla extract
1	(¼-ounce) packet RapidRise yeast	½	teaspoon ground cinnamon
2	cups all-purpose flour	¼	teaspoon ground nutmeg
6	tablespoons Duke's Mayonnaise		Cinnamon-Sugar Coating (recipe follows)

Recipe Continues

1. Heat the milk in a small saucepan to 120°F to 130°F. Stir in the sugar and yeast. Remove from the heat and let stand for 5 minutes, or until small bubbles appear on the surface.

2. Mix together the milk mixture, flour, mayonnaise, ¼ cup of the melted butter, the vanilla, cinnamon, and nutmeg in a medium bowl. Cover and refrigerate the batter overnight. (Or, cover and let stand at room temperature for 45 minutes, or until the batter rises and is doubled in bulk.)

3. Prepare the Cinnamon-Sugar Coating. Place the remaining ½ cup melted butter in a shallow bowl.

4. Remove the batter from the refrigerator, if applicable. Heat a waffle iron according to manufacturer's instructions. Add batter by ¼ cupfuls to the iron and cook until done. Toss the waffles in the melted butter, then coat in the Cinnamon-Sugar Coating.

CINNAMON-SUGAR Coating

Makes about 1 cup

1 CUP SUGAR

1 TABLESPOON GROUND CINNAMON

Mix together the sugar and cinnamon in a medium bowl.

TASTY TIP

Turn breakfast into an apple pie dessert.

These waffles are the perfect base for a scoop of vanilla ice cream topped with sautéed apples.

Easy

BUTTERMILK
Biscuits

MAKES 8 BISCUITS

Whether smeared with butter and preserves, drizzled with honey, or sandwiched with a sausage patty, these ultra-easy biscuits are my go-to breakfast staple. The Duke's makes them tender and flaky. Note that they are their best when all of the ingredients start out very cold.

2¼	cups self-rising soft wheat flour (such as White Lily)
¼	teaspoon baking powder
	Pinch of salt
½	cup cold Duke's Mayonnaise
¾	cup cold whole buttermilk
	Melted butter, for brushing

1. Combine the flour, baking powder, and salt in a large bowl. Add the mayonnaise and mix with a fork until the mixture resembles coarse crumbs. Refrigerate for 15 minutes.

2. Preheat the oven to 475°F. Line a rimmed baking sheet with parchment paper.

3. Remove the flour mixture from the refrigerator. Stir in the buttermilk just until the dough is moistened and comes together. Turn out onto a lightly floured surface. Roll out the dough and fold it into thirds (like an envelope), then repeat the process three times. (This will create layers.) Roll the dough to a ¾-inch thickness. Cut out rounds with a floured 2-inch biscuit cutter, rerolling as needed, and place on the prepared baking sheet.

4. Brush the tops of the biscuits with melted butter. Bake the biscuits at 475°F for 10 to 11 minutes, until golden brown on the bottoms. If desired, turn on the broiler and broil for 30 seconds for golden brown tops.

TASTY TIP

For ultimate flaky layers, don't skip the step of folding the dough like an envelope.

HAM, MUSHROOM, *and* Comté Omelets

MAKES 4 SERVINGS

I had never heard of Comté cheese until my culinary school friend Nicki, who worked with the Comté Cheese Association, asked that I join her on a press trip to the Jura region of France to learn about it. The whole process of making the cheese was magical to me: The cow's milk is collected from many different farms, and the flavor of the milk is impacted significantly by what the cows eat—hay in the winter, and grassland and flowers in the spring and summer. A wheel of Comté made from winter milk will taste buttery, while spring milk gives it more floral notes. The nuttiness of the cheese is the perfect complement to ham and mushrooms in these omelets, and the Duke's makes the omelets perfectly fluffy. But the flavor is not the only thing I love about Comté: I arrived in France the week before that press trip for some solo travel, when I was surprised by the appearance of Chris, who then proposed.

6	tablespoons salted butter, divided
1	(8-ounce) package sliced mushrooms
1	clove garlic, minced
¼	teaspoon salt, plus more to season
¼	teaspoon freshly ground pepper, plus more to season
12	large eggs
6	tablespoons Duke's Mayonnaise
1	teaspoon Dijon mustard
1	cup shredded Comté cheese (or use Gruyère)
½	pound thinly sliced or chopped deli ham
	Watercress (optional)

1. Melt 2 tablespoons of the butter in a large skillet over medium-high heat. Add the mushrooms, garlic, salt, and pepper. Sauté for 5 to 6 minutes, until the mushrooms are browned. Set aside.

2. For each omelet, whisk together 3 eggs, 1½ tablespoons mayonnaise, and ¼ teaspoon mustard.

3. Melt 1 tablespoon of the butter in a small nonstick skillet over medium-high heat. Add one portion of the egg mixture and let stand for 1 minute, or until the eggs begin to cook. Gently lift the edges of the eggs with a spatula and allow the uncooked egg to flow underneath. Continue the process until the eggs begin to set.

4. Once the eggs are almost set, sprinkle ¼ cup of the cheese onto half of the eggs; top with one-fourth of the ham and one-fourth of the sautéed mushrooms. Carefully lift the untopped egg half over the filling, and press with the spatula to seal.

5. Slide the omelet onto a serving plate and sprinkle with salt and pepper to taste.

6. Repeat the process with the remaining ingredients to make 4 omelets. Garnish the omelets with watercress, if desired.

I'm a California boy and grew up with another celebrated brand of mayonnaise popular on the West Coast. When I moved to Virginia, I found that my brand was unavailable, and I became aware of all this fuss about Duke's Mayonnaise. Every Southern chef out here glorified Duke's, and every recipe, it seemed, didn't just mention "mayonnaise" as an ingredient but specifically asked that Duke's be used. I grabbed a jar, dove in, and really loved its creaminess and purity, and I became hooked. I became one of *those* chefs, and in my new *Red Truck Bakery Cookbook,* I mention that our jalapeño mayonnaise and Mexican crab cakes should be made with Duke's—its pure flavor doesn't muddy any added ingredients, and (in this case) the fresh green jalapeño and cilantro flavors come through, carried cleanly by the Duke's Mayonnaise. And in my book's introduction, going full circle back to my California days, I open with an anecdote about the time actor John Wayne taught me to make a tuna sandwich his way in his Newport Beach kitchen—and when it came to his mayonnaise, I sure hoped (for a variety of reasons) that he used Duke's. We make that sandwich every day at our two stores, and we only use Duke's. I won't use anything else, and I think that the Duke would agree.

John Wayne made me a tuna sandwich. I was the 19-year-old art director at a weekly newspaper in Corona del Mar, California, and had an appointment with actor John Wayne's housekeeper to return some photos we used in a profile on him. I went out at lunch time, stopping first to have a burger, then walked up to his door holding the heavy box of framed photos. Nearly dropping it, I kicked the door several times with my foot (hey, I was only 19). The door was yanked open and Wayne himself answered, scowling at me. I handed him the box of photos, apologized, and was invited in. "Ya wanna tuna sandwich?" he asked. Even though I had just eaten, I wasn't going to pass that up. He led me through the estate overlooking Newport Bay, and we ended up in the kitchen with a view of his yacht, the Wild Goose. He toasted hearty slices of wheat bread, then spread each with mayonnaise (I like to think it was Duke's). He made the tuna salad with a good pinch of salt to boost the flavor, chopped up sweet pickles and celery, and mixed it all up with a big spoonful of more mayo, plopping a big mound onto a pile of lettuce. Before adding the top slice of bread, he smashed his fistful of potato chips into the tuna filling, commanding in his drawl, "This is why you'll like this." I've made it the same way ever since. John Wayne's lesson sticks with me forty years later: There are no rules. Put your own personal creative spin on food and be confident enough of the results to offer it up to others.

—BRIAN NOYES, FOUNDER AND BAKER-IN-CHIEF, RED TRUCK BAKERY IN MARSHALL, VIRGINIA

Bananas Foster
Bread

with BROWNED BUTTER–RUM GLAZE

MAKES 8 SERVINGS

~ ~

You want to know the secret to this scrumptious banana bread—besides the Duke's, of course, that makes it extra moist? It's letting your bananas get so ripe that you almost think you have to throw them out. Super-ripe bananas lend that desirable banana-y flavor. My son gets on banana kicks where he can eat several a day. I get to the point of buying bunches of them a couple of times a week. Then, all of a sudden, he decides he doesn't want them anymore. And I'm left with bananas turning black on the counter. That's when I make this New Orleans–inspired loaf.

~ ~

1½	cups mashed very ripe banana (3 to 4 large bananas)
¾	cup firmly packed light brown sugar
¼	cup salted butter, melted
1	large egg
⅔	cup Duke's Mayonnaise
3	tablespoons golden or dark rum

1	teaspoon vanilla extract
1½	cups all-purpose flour
1	teaspoon baking soda
½	teaspoon salt
½	teaspoon ground cinnamon
1	banana, sliced lengthwise
	Browned Butter–Rum Glaze (recipe follows)

Recipe Continues

1. Preheat the oven to 350°F. Grease a 9- x 5-inch loaf pan (I use vegetable shortening).

2. Beat together the mashed bananas, brown sugar, butter, egg, mayonnaise, rum, and vanilla in a large bowl with an electric mixer until smooth.

3. Mix together the flour, baking soda, salt, and cinnamon in a medium bowl. Add to the banana mixture and stir just until combined.

4. Pour the batter into the prepared pan. Top with the sliced banana, cut sides up. Bake the bread at 350°F for 1 hour and 5 minutes, or until a toothpick inserted in the center comes out clean.

5. Let the bread cool in the pan on a wire rack. Make the Browned Butter–Rum Glaze while the bread cools.

6. Remove the bread from the pan and drizzle with the Browned Butter–Rum Glaze.

TASTY TIP

For easy mashing, place peeled bananas in a large zip-top plastic bag.

Seal the bag and press on the bananas until mashed. Snip the corner of the bag and squeeze into a measuring cup.

BROWNED BUTTER-RUM *Glaze*

Makes about ½ cup

2 TABLESPOONS SALTED BUTTER

2 TABLESPOONS GOLDEN OR DARK RUM

½ CUP POWDERED SUGAR

1. Cook the butter in a small skillet over medium heat for 2 to 3 minutes, swirling the pan occasionally, until the milk solids begin to brown and smell nutty.

2. Remove the pan from the heat and carefully stir in the rum. Return to the heat and cook for 30 seconds to 1 minute longer to cook off the alcohol. (If using a gas burner, carefully flambé the mixture.) Transfer the glaze to a small bowl and whisk in the sugar until smooth.

SUN-DRIED TOMATO, GOAT CHEESE, *and* SPINACH

Quiche

MAKES 6 TO 8 SERVINGS

You'll find Duke's in both the crust and the filling of this quiche. One taste of the crust and you'll wonder why you haven't been putting mayonnaise in pie crust all along. It creates an ideal flaky texture. Making it in a food processor also helps prevent over-mixing. The filling has one of my favorite ingredients: sun-dried tomatoes. I like to use some of the flavorful oil from the jar for sautéing the spinach, but you can use olive oil instead.

	Flaky Pie Dough (recipe follows)
1	tablespoon oil from the sun-dried tomato jar (or use olive oil)
1	clove garlic, minced
1	(5-ounce) package baby spinach
½	cup julienned oil-packed sun-dried tomatoes
4	large eggs
½	cup Duke's Mayonnaise

½	cup whole milk
½	cup freshly grated Asiago or Parmesan cheese
¼	cup chopped fresh basil, plus more for garnish (optional)
½	teaspoon salt
½	teaspoon freshly ground pepper
1	(4-ounce) log goat cheese, crumbled

Recipe Continues

1. Make the Flaky Pie Dough.

2. Preheat the oven to 400°F.

3. Roll out the Flaky Pie Dough to a ¼-inch thickness. Fit into a 9-inch pie plate or tin; fold the edges under and crimp. Fill the pie shell with parchment paper and dried beans or pie weights. Bake at 400°F for 12 minutes, or until the crust is baked through. Remove the pie crust from the oven and let cool. Reduce the oven temperature to 350°F.

4. Heat the oil in a large nonstick skillet over medium-high heat. Add the garlic and spinach and cook for 2 to 3 minutes, until the spinach wilts.

5. Spread the spinach mixture and tomatoes evenly in the pre-baked pie crust. Whisk together the eggs, mayonnaise, milk, Asiago cheese, basil, salt, and pepper in a medium bowl. Pour over the spinach mixture.

6. Dot the filling with the goat cheese. Bake the quiche at 350°F for 40 minutes, or until the quiche is set. Let cool on a wire rack before cutting into wedges. Garnish with basil leaves, if desired.

TASTY TIP

For a gluten-free version,

make a frittata instead: Simply pour the filling into a skillet or ovenproof dish (omitting the crust) and bake until done.

Flaky PIE DOUGH

Makes enough dough for 1 (9-inch) crust

2 CUPS ALL-PURPOSE FLOUR

½ TEASPOON SALT

½ CUP DUKE'S MAYONNAISE

¼ CUP COLD WATER

Pulse the flour, salt, and mayonnaise in a food processor until crumbly. Gradually add the cold water through the food chute and pulse just until the dough comes together. Shape into a disk and let rest at room temperature for 30 minutes. (Or, refrigerate until ready to use and let stand at room temperature for 1 hour or until pliable.)

Earl Grey
Scones

MAKES 8 SCONES

~ ~

When I was in high school, my parents bought a historic home in downtown Savannah and turned it into a bed and breakfast called The Hamilton-Turner Inn. Conveniently, I was of working age, so after school I would help serve afternoon tea to guests. This was where my love of cooking really blossomed, and one of my favorite things to make and serve were scones, served with Earl Grey tea of course. Here, I've married the two to result in a tender, tea-kissed scone that is perfect for breakfast (or afternoon tea).

~ ~

2¾	cups self-rising soft wheat flour (such as White Lily)
2	tablespoons granulated sugar
1	tablespoon loose Earl Grey tea (from about 3 tea bags)
⅓	cup Duke's Mayonnaise
1	cup whole buttermilk
1	large egg
1	teaspoon water
	Earl Grey Glaze (recipe follows)

1. Preheat the oven to 425°F. Line a rimmed baking sheet with parchment paper.

2. Stir together the flour, granulated sugar, and tea in a medium bowl. Add the mayonnaise and cut in with two forks until the mayonnaise is incorporated and the mixture is sandy.

3. Gradually add the buttermilk, stirring with a fork until the dough comes together but is still shaggy. With floured hands, turn the dough out onto the prepared baking sheet and shape into a round about ½ inch thick.

Recipe Continues

4. Whisk together the egg and water in a small bowl; brush an even coat of the egg wash over the dough. Using a floured chef's knife or pastry scraper, cut the dough into 8 equal wedges, cleaning the knife after each cut if necessary. (Keep the dough in a round instead of separating.)

5. Bake the scones at 425°F for 13 to 15 minutes, until a toothpick inserted in the thickest portion comes out clean.

6. While the scones bake, make the Earl Grey Glaze. Let the scones cool slightly, then cut or break into wedges. Drizzle with Earl Grey Glaze.

TASTY TIP

After the scones have baked, turn on the broiler and broil the scones for 30 seconds to brown the tops, if desired.

EARL GREY
Glaze

Makes about ¾ cup

¼ CUP WHOLE MILK

1 EARL GREY TEA BAG

1½ CUPS POWDERED SUGAR

1. Place the milk and tea bag in a small saucepan over medium-high heat and bring to a boil. Remove the pan from the heat and let the tea steep for 5 minutes. Squeeze the tea bag and remove from the milk. Let cool slightly.

2. Whisk together the steeped milk and powdered sugar in a medium bowl until smooth.

TASTY TIP

Because it's such a small amount of milk, you may want to pour the simmering milk and tea bag into a measuring cup or tea cup to allow the tea bag to steep while completely immersed in the hot liquid.

Peaches and Cream Crêpes

MAKES 18 FILLED CRÊPES

	Peach Topping (recipe follows)
2	cups all-purpose flour
2	tablespoons granulated sugar
2	cups whole milk
3	tablespoons Duke's Mayonnaise
2	large eggs
1	teaspoon vanilla extract
	Sweet Cream Filling (recipe follows)
	Vegetable oil, for the pan

I love a crêpe. In high school, I was president of the French club and was in charge of bringing the crêpes to our parties. The trick to making them is getting the pan hot and making sure the batter is thin enough to spread into an even, almost transparent layer in the pan. I like to make the Peach Topping before I make the crêpes to allow the peaches to macerate and create a juicy sauce. If it's the peak of peach season, you won't need all of the sugar in the peach topping.

1. Prepare the Peach Topping.

2. Combine the flour and granulated sugar in a small bowl.

3. Whisk together the milk, mayonnaise, eggs, and vanilla in a large bowl. Add the flour mixture and whisk until smooth. (The batter will be thin.) Cover and refrigerate for 30 minutes.

4. While the batter chills, prepare the Sweet Cream Filling.

5. Heat a lightly greased large nonstick skillet over medium-high heat until hot. Pour about ⅓ cup of the batter into the skillet, and tilt the skillet in a circular motion to create a very thin round pancake. Cook for 1 to 2 minutes on each side, until lightly browned. (The batter will set and will be easy to lift around the edges; bubbles will form underneath.) Remove to a plate and repeat the process with the remaining batter to make about 18 crêpes.

6. To serve, spread the Sweet Cream Filling evenly on the crêpes. Fold the crêpes in half and in half again. Top evenly with the Peach Topping.

Recipe Continues

Peach TOPPING

Makes about 4 cups

4 LARGE PEACHES, PITTED AND SLICED

2 TO 3 TABLESPOONS GRANULATED SUGAR

1 TEASPOON FRESH LEMON JUICE

Toss together all the ingredients in a medium bowl. Let stand for 1 hour at room temperature to allow the peach juices to release.

TASTY TIP

If peaches aren't in season, you can use frozen. Or, instead of the cream filling, just smear the crêpes with Nutella for a classic French treat.

Sweet Cream FILLING

Makes about 2 cups

1 (8-OUNCE) BLOCK CREAM CHEESE, SOFTENED

$\frac{1}{4}$ CUP POWDERED SUGAR

$\frac{3}{4}$ CUP WHIPPING CREAM

$\frac{1}{2}$ TEASPOON VANILLA EXTRACT

In a medium bowl, beat the cream cheese with an electric mixer until creamy. Add the powdered sugar, cream, and vanilla and beat until fluffy.

Cinnamon Rolls

with CREAM CHEESE GLAZE

MAKES 1 DOZEN ROLLS

~ ~ ~ ~ ~ ~ ~ ~ ~ ~ ~ ~ ~ ~

These cinnamon rolls are so good—you may have trouble eating just one. Duke's makes the dough really nice to work with and yields a tender bread. You can prep these the day before so they are ready to bake for brunch the next day. After you cut the dough into rolls and place them in the baking pan, cover and refrigerate overnight.

~ ~ ~ ~ ~ ~ ~ ~ ~ ~ ~ ~ ~ ~

1	cup whole milk
1	(¼-ounce) packet active dry yeast
½	cup granulated sugar, divided
3¾ to 4	cups all-purpose flour, divided, plus more for dusting
¼	cup Duke's Mayonnaise
5	tablespoons salted butter, melted, divided
	Pinch of salt
1	teaspoon vanilla extract
	Cinnamon Filling (recipe follows)
	Cream Cheese Glaze (recipe follows)

1. Heat the milk to 110°F to 115°F in a small saucepan over medium heat. Stir in the yeast and 1 tablespoon of the granulated sugar. Remove from the heat and let stand for 5 minutes, or until bubbles appear on the surface.

2. Combine the milk mixture, the remaining sugar, ½ cup of the flour, the mayonnaise, 4 tablespoons of the butter, the salt, and vanilla in the bowl of a heavy stand mixer. Add more flour, ½ cup at a time, beating until the dough comes together and begins to pull away from the sides of the bowl. (The dough will be slightly sticky.)

3. Turn the dough out onto a lightly floured surface and knead with floured hands for 10 minutes, or until the dough is smooth and elastic and springs back when pressed. Place the dough in an oiled bowl, cover, and let rise in a warm place, free from drafts, for 2 hours or until doubled in bulk.

4. While the dough rises, prepare the Cinnamon Filling.

5. Punch the dough down and shape into a rectangle on a lightly floured surface. Roll the dough out into an 18- x 12-inch rectangle. Spread the Cinnamon Filling evenly over the top of the dough. Starting with the long side, roll the dough up into a tight log. Trim the ends, if desired, then cut into 12 equal rolls.

6. Arrange the rolls in a greased 13- x 9-inch baking pan. Cover and let rise for 2 hours or until doubled in bulk. (Or, cover and refrigerate overnight. Remove from the refrigerator and let rise at room temperature until doubled in bulk, about 3 hours.)

7. Preheat the oven to 350°F. Brush the rolls with the remaining 1 tablespoon melted butter. Bake for 22 minutes, or until the rolls are browned and the centers are done.

8. While the rolls bake, prepare the Cream Cheese Glaze. Spread the rolls with the Cream Cheese Glaze while still warm.

Recipe Continues

Cinnamon FILLING

Makes about 1 cup

½ CUP SALTED BUTTER, MELTED

½ CUP FIRMLY PACKED LIGHT BROWN SUGAR

½ CUP GRANULATED SUGAR

2 TABLESPOONS GROUND CINNAMON

Stir together all the ingredients in a small bowl.

Cream Cheese GLAZE

Makes about 2¼ cups

1 (8-OUNCE) BLOCK CREAM CHEESE, SOFTENED

2 TEASPOONS VANILLA EXTRACT

3 CUPS POWDERED SUGAR

2 TABLESPOONS WHIPPING CREAM

Combine all the ingredients in a medium bowl and beat with an electric mixer until smooth.

Anyone who knows me knows that mayonnaise is my favorite food on earth. Calling it a condiment is a travesty, when the truth is that it is the one and only true mother sauce. I come from the North, which unfortunately means that I was graced by the presence of the almighty Duke's a bit later in life. That's OK though. I'm making up for lost time by deploying it in my life any chance I get. That pale-yellow color lets you know that they don't skimp on the yolks. The extra viscosity that comes from a slow and patient emulsion process. The extra two ounces that all the other companies seemed to cheat us out of. I love you, Duke's.

—ALEX STUPAK, CHEF AND OWNER OF
EMPELLÓN IN NEW YORK, NEW YORK

OLD-FASHIONED
Doughnuts
with MIXED BERRY GLAZE

MAKES 14 DOUGHNUTS AND HOLES

~ ~ ~ ~ ~ ~ ~ ~ ~ ~ ~ ~ ~ ~ ~ ~ ~ ~ ~ ~

I've always loved doughnuts, but I didn't really indulge in them until I had a toddler. One of our favorite weekend traditions when we lived in Florida was to go to Donut Circus on Saturday mornings so my little guy could get a pink-frosted doughnut with "minkles" (sprinkles). That tradition was my inspiration for these delicious treats. The mayonnaise in the doughnut dough yields a tender crumb, and the pink-hued mixed berry glaze is well worth the effort. We don't like berry seeds in my family, so I opt to strain them out. If they don't bother you, skip the straining for a more rustic glaze.

~ ~ ~ ~ ~ ~ ~ ~ ~ ~ ~ ~ ~ ~ ~ ~ ~ ~ ~ ~

	Mixed Berry Glaze (recipe follows)	½	teaspoon baking soda
1	large egg	1	teaspoon ground nutmeg
1	cup granulated sugar	1	teaspoon ground cinnamon
¼	cup Duke's Mayonnaise	¾	cup whole milk
4¼	cups all-purpose flour, plus more for dusting	1	teaspoon vanilla extract
2	teaspoons baking powder		Vegetable oil, for frying
			Sprinkles (optional)

1. Make the Mixed Berry Glaze. Set aside.

2. Beat the egg, granulated sugar, and mayonnaise in the bowl of a heavy stand mixer until creamy.

3. Stir together the flour, baking powder, baking soda, nutmeg, and cinnamon in a medium bowl. Add the flour mixture to the egg mixture alternately with the milk, beginning and ending with the flour mixture. Beat in the vanilla.

4. Pour oil to a depth of 1½ inches in a large Dutch oven. Heat to 350°F over medium-high heat.

5. Turn the dough out onto a lightly floured surface. Dust the dough with flour and roll out to a ½-inch thickness. Using a floured 2½-inch doughnut cutter, cut the dough into doughnuts and doughnut holes, coating the cutter with flour after each cut and rerolling the dough as needed. (If you don't have a doughnut cutter, use a 2½-inch biscuit cutter to cut out rounds, then use a 1-inch biscuit cutter to cut holes out of the centers.)

6. Fry the doughnuts and holes, in batches, for 2 to 3 minutes, turning occasionally to brown evenly. Drain on paper towels. Dip in the Mixed Berry Glaze, sprinkle with sprinkles, if desired, and let harden on a wire rack.

TASTY TIP

These are best served fresh, even slightly warm.

MIXED BERRY
Glaze

Makes 2 cups

1 CUP FROZEN MIXED BERRIES

2 TABLESPOONS FRESH LEMON JUICE

¼ CUP GRANULATED SUGAR

⅓ CUP SALTED BUTTER, MELTED

2 TO 3 CUPS POWDERED SUGAR

1. Bring the berries, lemon juice, and granulated sugar to a boil in a small saucepan. Simmer for 5 to 8 minutes, until the berries release their juices and the mixture becomes syrupy. Strain the berries to remove seeds if desired, pressing the berries with the back of a spoon to release as much juice as possible.

2. Add the butter and enough powdered sugar to make the glaze a good dipping consistency, stirring until smooth.

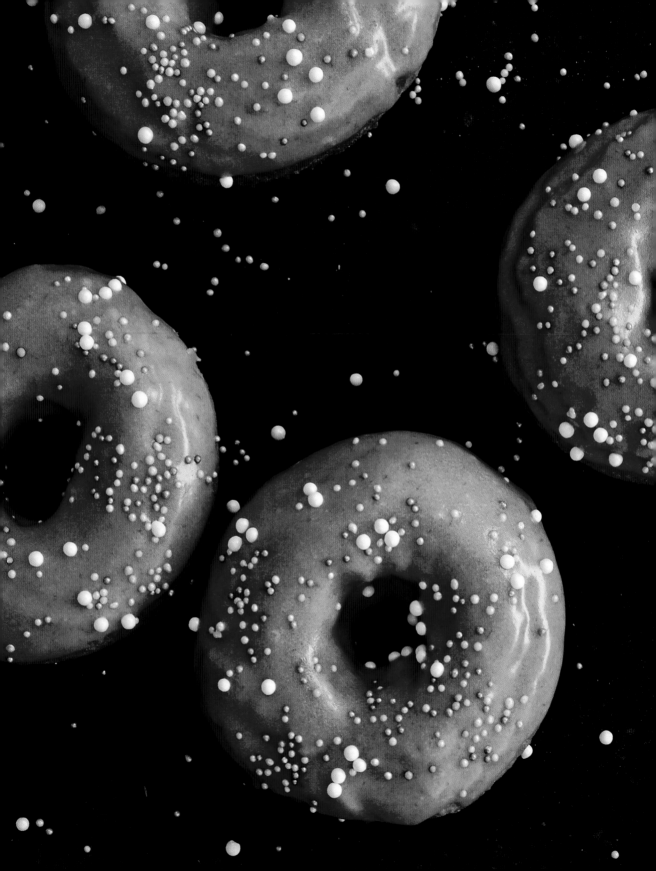

Old-Fashioned
Doughnuts with
Mixed Berry
Glaze,
PAGE 42

CHAPTER TWO

LUNCH

Salads, Soups, and Sandwiches

MEDITERRANEAN
Seafood Pasta Salad
66

Pork Banh Mi
WITH SPICY MAYO 81

GREEN TOMATO PIE
73

ULTIMATE GRILLED CHEESE SANDWICHES
WITH QUICK TOMATO SOUP 57

ISRAELI COUSCOUS
AND BROCCOLI SALAD 56

BOURRIDE (FISH STEW)
WITH AÏOLI 88

AVOCADO BLTs
with Basil Mayo 50

Lemony Herbed Egg Salad Sandwiches
60

Mile-High Bacon Cheeseburgers with Burger Sauce 79

MARINATED STEAK SALAD WITH CREAMY BUTTERMILK-HERB DRESSING 62

ROASTED BEET, ORANGE, AND FARRO SALAD WITH GREEN GODDESS DRESSING 69

OYSTER PO' BOYS WITH CREOLE RÉMOULADE 86

CURRIED CHICKEN SALAD SANDWICHES 53

CRAB AND LOBSTER ROLLS 85

BUFFALO CHICKEN SLIDERS WITH BLUE CHEESE SAUCE 74

AVOCADO
BLTs
with BASIL MAYO

MAKES 4 SANDWICHES

~~~~~~~~~~~~~~~~~~~~~~~~~~~~~~~~~~

Ripe summer tomatoes and Duke's are a match made in heaven. To me, there isn't a better sandwich out there, and family reunions growing up were incomplete if we didn't bring the tomato sandwiches. This recipe takes the humble tomato sandwich to a new level as a BLT—but with the addition of avocado and basil. And I don't just pop the bread slices in the toaster but slather them with Duke's before toasting in the oven to bake up to a gorgeous golden brown. The sandwiches are easy enough to enjoy during the week but with a twist to make lunch feel fancy.

~~~~~~~~~~~~~~~~~~~~~~~~~~~~~~~~~~

	Basil Mayo (recipe follows)
8	thick slices sourdough bread
¼	cup Duke's Mayonnaise
2	avocados, pitted, peeled, and sliced
2	tomatoes, sliced
8	slices bacon, cooked
4	butter lettuce leaves
¼	cup fresh basil leaves

1. Preheat the oven to 400°F. Make the Basil Mayo while the oven heats.

2. Brush one side of the bread slices with the mayonnaise and place, mayo side up, in a single layer on a rimmed baking sheet. Bake for 5 minutes, or until the bread is toasted.

3. Spread the Basil Mayo evenly on one side of each slice of toast. Top four slices evenly with sliced avocado, tomato, bacon, lettuce, and basil. Top with the remaining four slices, Basil Mayo sides down.

Recipe Continues

Basil MAYO

Makes about ²/₃ cup

¹/₂ CUP DUKE'S MAYONNAISE

¹/₄ CUP CHOPPED FRESH BASIL

1 CLOVE GARLIC, MINCED

Stir together all the ingredients in a small bowl. Refrigerate until ready to serve or up to 2 days.

How is it that one of the world's greatest sandwiches—the BLT—leaves out the letter, which in my opinion, is the whole reason the sandwich works. Everything is better with mayonnaise—especially Duke's.

—CHEF LINTON HOPKINS, HOPKINS AND COMPANY IN ATLANTA, GEORGIA

SHOWN ON PAGE 54

Curried
Chicken Salad
SANDWICHES

MAKES 4 SANDWICHES

I love a good chicken salad, and this version is probably my favorite. Shredded rotisserie chicken makes preparation a snap, and the flavors only get better with time if you make the salad ahead and refrigerate it until ready to serve. Instead of the baguettes you could serve the chicken salad on a bed of mixed greens.

1	rotisserie chicken, skin removed
½	cup finely chopped celery
½	cup chopped salted roasted pistachios
¼	cup chopped fresh flat-leaf parsley
2	green onions, chopped
1	cup dried sweetened cranberries
1	cup Duke's Mayonnaise
2	tablespoons honey
1	tablespoon curry powder
	Salt and freshly ground pepper
	Miniature baguettes
	Baby arugula

1. Using two forks or your fingers, shred the chicken into small pieces and place in a large bowl. (You should have about 4 cups pulled chicken.) Stir in the celery, pistachios, parsley, green onions, and cranberries.

2. Stir together the mayonnaise, honey, and curry powder in a small bowl. Pour the desired amount of dressing over the chicken mixture and toss to coat well. Season with salt and pepper to taste. Refrigerate until ready to serve or up to 2 days.

3. Serve the chicken salad on baguettes with baby arugula.

TASTY TIP

Shred the chicken while it's still warm; it's much easier!

Israeli Couscous and Broccoli Salad, PAGE 56

Curried Chicken Salad Sandwiches, PAGE 53

Lemony Herbed Egg Salad Sandwiches, PAGE 60

Mediterranean Seafood Pasta Salad, PAGE 66

SHOWN ON PAGE 54

Israeli Couscous

AND BROCCOLI SALAD

MAKES 4 SERVINGS

I love traditional broccoli salad; the crunchy broccoli with tangy dressing, sweet cranberries, and crisp bacon tempt every taste bud. This is an update of that salad, with couscous and chickpeas added to make it a more filling, main-dish salad. This is a great recipe to make ahead and tote to work too.

1	tablespoon olive oil
1	cup uncooked Israeli couscous
1½	cups water
¼	teaspoon salt
1	(12-ounce) package broccoli florets
1	shallot, minced
¾	cup Duke's Mayonnaise
2	tablespoons honey
1	tablespoon apple cider vinegar
½	cup sliced almonds, toasted
½	cup golden raisins
1	(15.5-ounce) can chickpeas, rinsed and drained
4	slices bacon, cooked and crumbled (optional)
	Salt and freshly ground pepper

1. Heat the oil in a medium saucepan over medium heat. Add the couscous and cook for 1 to 2 minutes, until the couscous is toasted. Add the water and salt and bring to a boil. Cover, reduce the heat, and simmer over low heat for 10 to 12 minutes, until the liquid is absorbed. Rinse with cold water to cool; drain.

2. While the couscous cooks, bring a pot of salted water to a boil. Fill a bowl with ice and water. Add the broccoli to the boiling water and cook for 2 to 3 minutes, until the broccoli is bright green and crisp-tender. Drain and immediately plunge in the ice water to stop cooking. Drain.

3. Whisk together the shallot, mayonnaise, honey, and vinegar in a large bowl. Add the couscous, broccoli, almonds, raisins, chickpeas, and bacon, if using. Toss well to combine. Season with salt and pepper to taste. Serve immediately or cover and refrigerate until ready to serve or up to 2 days.

Ultimate
Grilled Cheese
SANDWICHES
with QUICK TOMATO SOUP

MAKES 4 SERVINGS

Move over butter: Mayo is the way to go to make the perfect crispy-crusted grilled cheese. Depending on the size of the loaf you buy, you may need a couple of teaspoons to up to a tablespoon of mayonnaise to brush an even coat on each slice of the bread. I like to use a good sharp white Cheddar cheese, such as Kerrygold, but feel free to use any sharp Cheddar you'd like. These sandwiches are great on their own, but the perfect complement is tomato soup. I've included a quick recipe that's so much better than canned and well worth it. I make the soup first (or even the day before) and keep it warm on the stove while I make the sandwiches.

8	slices bakery sourdough bread
8	slices sharp Irish or English Cheddar cheese
8	slices Muenster cheese
¼ to ½	cup Duke's Mayonnaise
	Quick Tomato Soup (recipe follows, optional)

1. Arrange four bread slices on a clean work surface. Top each slice with two slices Cheddar and two slices Muenster cheese. Top with the remaining bread slices.

2. Spread the mayonnaise on the tops of each sandwich. Place a large nonstick skillet over medium heat until hot. Invert the sandwiches into the skillet and spread the mayonnaise onto the other sides. Cook the sandwiches for 2 minutes on each side, or until the bread is golden brown and the cheese is melted. Serve with Quick Tomato Soup, if desired.

Recipe Continues

Quick TOMATO SOUP

Makes 4 servings

1 TABLESPOON OLIVE OIL

1 ONION, CHOPPED

2 CARROTS, CHOPPED

3 CLOVES GARLIC, MINCED

1/4 TEASPOON RED PEPPER FLAKES

1 (28-OUNCE) CAN PEELED
WHOLE SAN MARZANO TOMATOES
(UNDRAINED), CHOPPED

1 3/4 CUPS VEGETABLE BROTH

1/2 CUP HEAVY CREAM

1/2 TEASPOON SALT

FRESH BASIL (OPTIONAL)

1. Heat the oil in a large saucepan or Dutch oven over medium-high heat. Add the onion, carrots, garlic, and red pepper flakes and sauté for 5 to 6 minutes, until tender.

2. Add the tomatoes and broth. Simmer for 10 minutes, or until the soup is slightly reduced. Use an immersion blender to puree the soup to desired consistency. Or, puree the soup in batches in a traditional stand blender. (Be sure to remove the center of the blender top to allow steam to escape while blending.)

3. Add the cream and salt and simmer for 3 minutes, or until the soup is thickened. Sprinkle with fresh basil, if desired.

TASTY TIP

To easily chop the tomatoes without making a mess, open the can and use kitchen shears to cut them directly in the can.

SHOWN ON PAGE 55

Lemony
Herbed Egg Salad
SANDWICHES

MAKES 4 SANDWICHES

~~~~~~~~~~~~~~~~~~~~~~~~~~~~~~~~~~

I used to be indifferent to egg salad: Sure, it was a great way to use up those leftover boiled eggs from Easter and it is *the* sandwich you had to try if you went to the Master's. That was until I made this egg salad—a version different from the mushy pickle-laden salad I was used to. It's really quite a simple recipe, especially if you buy the already hard-boiled eggs from the deli section at your grocery store. Creamy Duke's is kicked up a notch with tangy lemon and fresh herbs. Spread on pumpernickel bread with sliced radishes and green leaf lettuce, you have a sandwich worthy to serve at the neighborhood bistro.

~~~~~~~~~~~~~~~~~~~~~~~~~~~~~~~~~~

8	large eggs
1	teaspoon baking soda
½	cup chopped celery
2	tablespoons minced red onion
2	tablespoons chopped fresh dill
2	tablespoons chopped fresh flat-leaf parsley
2	tablespoons chopped fresh chives
⅓	cup Duke's Mayonnaise
2	teaspoons yellow mustard
1	teaspoon grated lemon zest
1	teaspoon fresh lemon juice
¼	teaspoon salt
¼	teaspoon freshly ground pepper
8	slices pumpernickel bread
4	green leaf lettuce leaves
1	cup thinly sliced radishes

1. Place the eggs in a medium saucepan of cold water to cover. Add the baking soda and bring the water to a boil over high heat. Once boiling, remove the pan from the heat and cover the pan. Let stand for 12 minutes.

2. Fill a bowl with ice and water. Drain the eggs and plunge in the ice water bath. Let stand until cool.

3. Peel and chop the eggs, and place in a medium bowl. Add the celery, onion, dill, parsley, and chives.

4. Stir together the mayonnaise, mustard, lemon zest, lemon juice, salt, and pepper in a small bowl. Pour the dressing over the egg mixture and stir gently to combine.

5. Divide the egg salad evenly between four slices of bread; top with lettuce, sliced radishes, and the remaining bread slices.

TASTY TIP

Do you dread peeling eggs?

Besides using eggs that have been in your fridge for a little while, the baking soda in the boiling water should make them easier to peel.

Marinated

Steak Salad

with CREAMY BUTTERMILK-HERB DRESSING

MAKES 4 SERVINGS

This salad has elements that you can enjoy separately or together. The marinade for the steak is a little salty and a little sweet and so easy to put together. And, the dressing is a homemade version of ranch—perfect to drizzle on salad or serve as a dip with cut raw vegetables, roasted potatoes, or grilled chicken.

1½	pounds boneless top sirloin steak or flank steak
2	tablespoons packed light brown sugar
2	tablespoons balsamic vinegar
2	tablespoons reduced-sodium soy sauce
3	tablespoons olive oil, divided
1	tablespoon Worcestershire sauce
¼	teaspoon red pepper flakes

	Creamy Buttermilk-Herb Dressing (recipe follows)
2	ears corn, shucked and cleaned
1	head romaine lettuce, chopped
1	(5-ounce) package mixed baby greens
1	pint grape tomatoes, halved
1	English cucumber, cut into bite-size pieces
3	cups croutons (see Note)

Recipe Continues

1. Place the steak in a large zip-top plastic bag or large shallow dish. Whisk together the brown sugar, vinegar, soy sauce, 2 tablespoons of the olive oil, the Worcestershire sauce, and red pepper flakes. Pour over the steak and turn to coat. Seal the bag or cover the dish and refrigerate for at least 2 hours or up to 4 hours.

2. While the steak marinates, prepare the Creamy Buttermilk-Herb Dressing. Preheat the grill to medium-high heat. Remove the steak from the marinade and discard the marinade. Grill the steak, covered with the grill lid, for 5 to 6 minutes on each side, or to desired degree of doneness. Remove the steak from the grill to a cutting board and let rest for 10 minutes, then thinly slice against the grain.

3. While the steak cooks, brush the corn with the remaining 1 tablespoon olive oil. Grill the corn, covered with the grill lid, for 12 to 15 minutes, turning occasionally, until the corn is charred and tender. Remove the corn from the grill and let stand until cool enough to touch. Cut the kernels off the cobs.

4. To assemble the salad, toss together the romaine, mixed greens, corn, tomatoes, cucumber, and croutons. Divide the salad among serving plates and top with the steak. Drizzle with desired amount of Creamy Buttermilk-Herb Dressing.

Note

Use your favorite store-bought croutons or make your own. For from-scratch croutons, use 3 cups cubed bakery bread (day-old or stale bread works best). Toss with 1 tablespoon olive oil and your favorite seasonings, such as grated Parmesan cheese or Italian seasoning. Place on a parchment paper–lined baking sheet and bake at 375°F for 15 minutes, turning occasionally, until the croutons are browned and crisp. Let cool.

TASTY TIP

A Bundt pan makes cutting corn off the cob easy and mess-free:

Stand the corn cob up in the center of the pan and cut the kernels off the cob with a sharp chef's knife. They will fall into the cake pan—instead of bouncing around on your counter!

CREAMY BUTTERMILK-HERB *Dressing*

Makes about 1¾ cups

½ CUP DUKE'S MAYONNAISE

½ CUP SOUR CREAM

½ CUP WHOLE BUTTERMILK

2 TEASPOONS CHOPPED FRESH DILL

2 TEASPOONS CHOPPED FRESH FLAT-LEAF PARSLEY

2 TEASPOONS CHOPPED FRESH CHIVES

1 TEASPOON FRESH LEMON JUICE

½ TEASPOON GARLIC POWDER

¼ TEASPOON SALT

½ TEASPOON FRESHLY GROUND PEPPER

Whisk together all the ingredients in a small bowl. Cover and refrigerate until ready to serve or up to 3 days.

Mediterranean

Seafood Pasta Salad

MAKES 6 TO 8 SERVINGS

Growing up in the Lowcountry, it was inevitable that I would end up loving shrimp. One of my favorite memories was heading out in my grandfather's (Dado's) johnboat with my dad, Uncle Tommy, sister, and cousins to the secret shrimp hole. We were all pretty young—I was probably 10 or 12—and the dads would throw their cast nets into the water and haul up pounds of shrimp. The kids' duty was to pinch the heads off the shrimp while being surrounded by them. It doesn't get fresher than that. I recommend using fresh wild-caught shrimp in this pasta salad. The sweet shrimp combined with calamari makes it really special. Frozen calamari (that's already cleaned!) is readily available, but feel free to use more shrimp, crab, or your favorite seafood in its stead.

1	(16-ounce) package penne pasta
½	pound cleaned calamari tubes and tentacles
1	pound peeled and deveined medium shrimp
1	pint cherry tomatoes, halved
1	cup kalamata olives, halved
¼	cup chopped fresh basil
¼	cup chopped fresh flat-leaf parsley
¼	cup drained capers
½	cup Duke's Mayonnaise
3	tablespoons olive oil
2	tablespoons fresh lemon juice
¼	teaspoon red pepper flakes
	Salt and freshly ground pepper

1. Cook the pasta in salted water according to package directions until al dente. Drain, then rinse under cold water to cool.

2. Place ice and water in a large bowl. Cut the calamari into rings; leave the tentacles whole.

3. Bring salted water to a boil in a large saucepan. Add the shrimp and cook for 2 minutes, or until almost done. Add the calamari and cook for 30 seconds longer. Drain the seafood and immediately plunge into the ice water to stop cooking. Drain.

4. Combine the pasta, seafood, tomatoes, olives, basil, parsley, and capers in a large serving bowl.

5. Whisk together the mayonnaise, oil, lemon juice, and red pepper flakes. Pour the dressing over the pasta and toss to coat. Season with salt and pepper to taste and serve immediately or cover and refrigerate until ready to serve or up to 2 days.

TASTY TIP

The trick to non-rubber-band-like calamari is to cook it briefly—only 30 seconds is plenty.

ROASTED BEET, ORANGE, *and*
Farro Salad

with GREEN GODDESS DRESSING

MAKES 4 TO 6 SERVINGS

~ ~

This is one of my favorite kitchen sink–style salads. The combination of sweet oranges, earthy roasted beets, nutty farro, creamy avocado, and a tangy herb dressing seems to satisfy whatever craving I have at any given time. The Green Goddess Dressing is also great to keep in the refrigerator as a sauce for chicken, pork, or seafood, or for an easy go-to dip for vegetables.

~ ~

2	bunches beets, peeled and cut into wedges
1	tablespoon olive oil
¼	teaspoon salt
¼	teaspoon freshly ground pepper
	Green Goddess Dressing (recipe follows)
2	cups farro
2	oranges, peeled and sectioned
2	avocados, pitted, peeled, and sliced
3	cups baby arugula

1. Preheat the oven to 425°F. Toss the beets with the oil, salt, and pepper on a rimmed baking sheet and roast, stirring occasionally, for 40 to 45 minutes, until the beets are tender. Remove from the oven and cool.

2. While the beets cook, prepare the Green Goddess Dressing and cook the farro according to package directions.

3. Arrange the beets, farro, oranges, avocado, and arugula on a serving platter. Drizzle with desired amount of dressing.

Recipe Continues

GREEN GODDESS
Dressing

Makes about 1¾ cups

2 CLOVES GARLIC, PEELED

³/₄ CUP DUKE'S MAYONNAISE

1 CUP FRESH FLAT-LEAF PARSLEY
LEAVES

¹/₄ CUP FRESH BASIL LEAVES

¹/₄ CUP CHOPPED FRESH CHIVES

3 TABLESPOONS FRESH LEMON JUICE

1 TABLESPOON WHITE WINE VINEGAR

¹/₄ CUP OLIVE OIL

¹/₄ TEASPOON SALT

¹/₄ TEASPOON FRESHLY GROUND
PEPPER

1. In a food processor, with the motor running, drop the garlic through the food chute and process until minced.

2. Remove the lid and add the remaining ingredients. Process until smooth. Cover and refrigerate until ready to serve or up to 3 days.

I love mayonnaise, and I've loved Duke's Mayo for as long as I can remember. When people asked if I had a favorite mayo, I said, "Duke's of course," just like all the other cool kids! But just last summer, I did my first real blind mayonnaise taste test over at the *Garden & Gun* office. I had never tasted Duke's side-by-side against other mayonnaise before! Of course, I picked Duke's! It tastes real, and it doesn't have sugar. It's the closest to what I would make if I were making mayo at home. We use it in all kinds of ways at Button & Co. Bagels— in the pimento cheese and chicken salad and on the pastrami sandwich. I use it in tomato pie at home. I love its savory quality!

—CHEF KATIE BUTTON

GREEN TOMATO Pie

MAKES 6 TO 8 SERVINGS

5	green tomatoes, sliced
1	teaspoon salt
	Flaky Pie Dough (see page 31)
1	cup shredded sharp white Cheddar cheese
1	cup freshly grated Parmesan cheese
¾	cup Duke's Mayonnaise
2	cloves garlic, minced
2	tablespoons chopped fresh basil, plus more for garnish (optional)
2	tablespoons chopped fresh flat-leaf parsley, plus more for garnish (optional)
2	tablespoons chopped fresh chives
¼	teaspoon freshly ground pepper

TASTY TIP

For a pretty presentation,

I like to add the final layer of tomatoes during the last 10 minutes of baking so they hold their shape. I also like to use a variety of heirloom green tomatoes, from green grape tomatoes to green zebra slicing tomatoes.

There are a lot of recipes out there for tomato pie, but they all use ripe red tomatoes. I love the tanginess of green tomatoes, and in this application they're heavenly. The combination of tart green tomatoes and a creamy filling of fresh basil, parsley, and chives, all baked in a flaky crust, yields the ultimate tomato pie.

1. Arrange the tomato slices in a single layer on paper towel–lined rimmed baking sheets. Sprinkle evenly with salt and let stand for 1 hour. Pat the tomatoes dry.

2. While the tomatoes stand, make the Flaky Pie Dough.

3. Preheat the oven to 375°F. Roll out the dough to a ¼-inch-thick round. Fit into a 9-inch pie plate or tin; fold the edges under and crimp. Prick the dough with a fork. Fill with parchment paper and dried beans or pie weights and bake at 375°F for 18 minutes, until the crust is baked through. Remove the crust from the oven. Reduce the oven temperature to 350°F.

4. Stir together the cheeses, mayonnaise, garlic, basil, parsley, chives, and pepper in a medium bowl.

5. Layer one-third of the tomatoes in a single layer on the bottom of the baked crust; top with half of the cheese mixture. Repeat layers. Top with the remaining tomatoes. Bake at 350°F for 30 minutes, or until the crust is browned and the filling is bubbly. Let rest for 10 minutes before slicing. Garnish with additional herbs, if desired.

Buffalo CHICKEN Sliders

with BLUE CHEESE SAUCE

MAKES 12 SLIDERS

When it comes to tailgating, it's all about the food (well, and maybe the adult beverages too). A pile of these little sandwiches is a crowd-pleaser and would be perfect to take to the pre-game party. Go Dawgs! They're also great for lunch; serve a few with pasta salad or chips. Be sure to buy ground chicken, not ground chicken breast. It's much easier to handle, and the burgers keep their shape better.

	Blue Cheese Sauce (recipe follows)
1½	pounds ground chicken
4	tablespoons Buffalo sauce, divided
1	tablespoon Duke's Mayonnaise
½	teaspoon garlic powder
1	tablespoon olive oil
12	slider buns
1	cup celery leaves
1	cup matchstick-cut carrots

1. Make the Blue Cheese Sauce.

2. Combine the ground chicken, 2 tablespoons of the Buffalo sauce, the mayonnaise, and garlic powder in a medium bowl. With wet hands, shape the mixture into 12 equal patties (the mixture will be sticky).

3. Heat the oil in a large nonstick skillet over medium-high heat. Cook the patties for 2 to 3 minutes on one side, until browned. Turn the patties and cook for 2 to 3 more minutes, until the burgers are done, basting with the remaining 2 tablespoons Buffalo sauce.

4. To serve, spread the Blue Cheese Sauce on the bun bottoms. Top with the burgers, then evenly with the celery leaves and carrots. Replace the bun tops and serve.

Recipe Continues

BLUE CHEESE
Sauce

Makes about 1 cup

$\frac{1}{2}$ CUP DUKE'S MAYONNAISE

$\frac{1}{2}$ CUP CRUMBLED BLUE CHEESE

1 TABLESPOON WHOLE MILK

1 TEASPOON WORCESTERSHIRE
SAUCE

$\frac{1}{4}$ TEASPOON PAPRIKA

Stir together all the ingredients in
a small bowl. Refrigerate until ready to
serve or up to 3 days.

Mayonnaise is a food group in the South. What other part of the country would combine pasta and mayonnaise and call it salad when the only vegetables in sight are onions and maybe a little celery? We may argue over the correct way to pronounce pecan and which BBQ sauce reigns supreme, but there's no argument when it comes to mayonnaise. We take our mayo pretty seriously—and if it's not homemade, it's got to be Duke's.

—VIRGINIA WILLIS, JAMES BEARD AWARD–WINNING COOKBOOK AUTHOR AND CHEF

Mile-High
Bacon Cheeseburgers

with BURGER SAUCE

MAKES 6 BURGERS

~ ~

My dad is the burger-grilling king. Whenever I'm home I request that he make them (and his famous spaghetti). But since I can't mimic his version, I've created my own, and I'm pretty sure you'll be the hero of any cookout when you grill up these juicy burgers. The secret is definitely in the sauce: It is so good you'll want to put it on everything—chicken fingers, French fries … a spoon.

~ ~

2	pounds ground round	1	red onion, sliced
¼	cup Duke's Mayonnaise	6	hamburger buns
1	tablespoon Worcestershire sauce	12	slices bacon, cooked
1	teaspoon garlic salt		Sandwich-sliced pickles
½	teaspoon freshly ground pepper		Tomato slices
	Burger Sauce (recipe follows)		Lettuce leaves
6	slices sharp Cheddar cheese		

Recipe Continues

1. Gently combine the ground round, mayonnaise, Worcestershire sauce, garlic salt, and pepper in a medium bowl. Shape the mixture into 6 (¾-inch-thick) patties.

2. Make the Burger Sauce.

3. Preheat the grill to medium-high heat. Grill the patties for 3 to 4 minutes on each side, until almost done. Place the cheese slices on the patties and let stand until melted.

4. While the burgers cook, grill the red onion slices alongside for 2 to 3 minutes on each side, until tender.

5. To serve, spread the Burger Sauce on the bun bottoms. Top with the patties, bacon, pickles, tomato, red onion, and lettuce. Replace the bun tops and serve immediately.

TASTY TIP

Make an indention in the center of each patty before grilling.

This helps the burgers keep a uniform shape while cooking.

BURGER *Sauce*

Makes about ¾ cup

½ CUP DUKE'S MAYONNAISE

2 TABLESPOONS HICKORY BBQ SAUCE

2 TABLESPOONS KETCHUP

1 TEASPOON YELLOW MUSTARD

½ TEASPOON PAPRIKA

Stir together all the ingredients in a small bowl. Refrigerate until ready to serve or up to 5 days.

PORK
Banh Mi
with SPICY MAYO

MAKES 4 SANDWICHES

1	pound ground pork
2	cloves garlic, minced
1	tablespoon minced fresh ginger
1	tablespoon finely chopped fresh basil
1	tablespoon Duke's Mayonnaise
1	tablespoon fish sauce
1	teaspoon cornstarch
1	green onion, minced
	Spicy Mayo (recipe follows)
	Vegetable Salad (recipe follows)
1	tablespoon vegetable oil
4	(4-ounce) French mini baguettes or hoagie rolls, split and toasted
2	jalapeños, sliced
¼	cup fresh cilantro leaves
¼	cup fresh basil leaves

The year we got married, my husband and I lived in Hong Kong for three months for his job, which meant weekends could be spent traveling around Asia. One of our most memorable trips was to Vietnam, and what I loved most about Hanoi and Ha Long Bay was the food. I couldn't get enough of steaming bowls of *bun cha* (chargrilled pork patties) soup and banh mi—French baguettes loaded down with sliced meat or meatballs, pickled vegetables, and lots of herbs. Here, Duke's acts as a binder and packs a punch of flavor in the meatballs. Mixed with sriracha, it also serves as a perfect sauce.

1. Mix together the ground pork, garlic, ginger, chopped basil, mayonnaise, fish sauce, cornstarch, and green onion. Shape into 16 (1-inch) balls.

2. Make the Spicy Mayo and the Vegetable Salad.

3. Heat the oil in a large skillet over medium-high heat. Add the meatballs and cook for 6 to 8 minutes, until browned on all sides.

4. To serve, spread the Spicy Mayo onto each roll. Top evenly with the meatballs, Vegetable Salad, jalapeños, cilantro leaves, and basil leaves. Serve immediately.

TASTY TIP

Wear gloves when slicing jalapeños to avoid mistakenly rubbing your eyes and causing burning.

Recipe Continues

Spicy
MAYO

Makes about ¾ cup

⅔ CUP DUKE'S MAYONNAISE

1 TABLESPOON SRIRACHA HOT SAUCE

Stir together the mayonnaise and sriracha in a small bowl. Refrigerate until ready to serve or up to 5 days.

Vegetable
SALAD

Makes about 3 cups

1 CUP SHREDDED CARROT

1 CUP THINLY SLICED RADISH

1 CUP THINLY SLICED CUCUMBER

2 TABLESPOONS RICE VINEGAR

2 TABLESPOONS GRANULATED SUGAR

1 TABLESPOON DARK SESAME OIL

Stir together all the ingredients in a medium bowl. Chill until ready to serve.

Crab *and* Lobster Rolls

MAKES 6 ROLLS

2	(1½-pound) Maine lobsters
1	pound lump crabmeat, picked through to remove any shells
½	cup finely chopped celery
1	teaspoon grated lemon zest
¼	cup fresh lemon juice
½	cup Duke's Mayonnaise
1	teaspoon Old Bay seasoning
¼	teaspoon paprika
	Pinch of cayenne pepper
3	tablespoons salted butter, divided
6	top-split brioche hot dog buns
	Boston lettuce leaves
	Chopped fresh chives
	Lemon wedges

I had my first lobster roll when I was an intern for *Coastal Living* magazine and working on a photo shoot. I immediately fell in love, and ever since, if there is a lobster roll on a menu, I have a tough time ordering anything else. You can't beat a buttered brioche bun piled high with creamy lobster salad. In this recipe, I add crabmeat to the mix—it adds a similar flavor but is less expensive and therefore stretches the filling a little further. Feel free to substitute shrimp for either the lobster or crab if you'd like. I also call for brioche hot dog buns, but you can use regular hot dog buns.

1. Fill a bowl with ice and water. Bring a large stockpot of water to a boil. Place the lobsters, heads first, into the water. Boil for 12 minutes, or until the lobsters are bright red. Plunge in the ice water to stop cooking.

2. Remove the lobster meat from the claws and tail. Cut into large chunks and place in a medium bowl. Toss in the crabmeat and celery.

3. Stir together the lemon zest, lemon juice, mayonnaise, Old Bay, paprika, and cayenne pepper in a small bowl. Pour the dressing over the lobster mixture and mix gently.

4. Melt 1 tablespoon of the butter in a large skillet. Add two buns, cut sides down, and cook for 30 seconds, until toasted. Repeat twice with the remaining butter and buns.

5. To serve, place the lettuce leaves in the buns. Top with the lobster mixture. Sprinkle with chives and serve with lemon wedges.

 **TASTY TIP**

If the lobsters are smaller or larger than the ones called for here, remember this rule of thumb: Boil the lobsters 7 minutes per pound for the first pound, and 3 minutes per pound thereafter. Or simply have your seafood monger steam the lobsters for you.

Oyster
Po' Boys
with CREOLE RÉMOULADE

MAKES 4 SANDWICHES

~ ~

Growing up in Savannah, Georgia, I am not a stranger to oysters. I would always look forward to the "-ber" months, when we could have oyster roasts. Whether chargrilled and placed atop a saltine with a squirt of Tabasco and lemon, fried until crisp, or shucked right out of the shell and slurped down with mignonette, I love the bivalve. Here, they are coated in a crisp cornmeal crust, fried, and gilded with a tangy mustard-mayonnaise sauce to star in the ultimate seafood sandwich. If you aren't a fan of oysters, shrimp work great too.

~ ~

1	(16-ounce) jar shucked oysters, drained		1	cup all-purpose flour
1	cup whole milk		1	teaspoon garlic powder
	Creole Rémoulade (recipe follows)		1	teaspoon salt, plus more if desired
3	tablespoons Duke's Mayonnaise		½	teaspoon cayenne pepper
2	tablespoons hot sauce			Vegetable oil, for frying
1	large egg		4	hoagie rolls, split
2	teaspoons water		1	cup shredded romaine lettuce
1	cup plain cornmeal		2	tomatoes, sliced
			½	cup dill pickle slices

1. Place the oysters in a medium bowl and cover with the milk. Refrigerate for 1 hour.

2. While the oysters chill, make the Creole Rémoulade.

3. Whisk together the mayonnaise, hot sauce, egg, and water in a medium bowl. Combine the cornmeal, flour, garlic powder, salt, and cayenne pepper in a brown paper bag.

4. Pour oil to a depth of 2 inches in a Dutch oven or heavy stockpot. Heat the oil to 365°F over medium-high heat. Place a rimmed baking sheet lined with paper towels beside the Dutch oven.

5. Drain the oysters and place in the egg mixture. Working one at a time, drop the oysters into the cornmeal mixture, shaking the bag gently after each oyster is added to distribute the coating evenly. Repeat the process until all the oysters are coated.

6. Fry the oysters, in batches, for 3 minutes, turning occasionally, until browned and crispy. Drain on the paper towels and sprinkle with additional salt if desired.

7. To serve, spread the Creole Rémoulade onto the hoagie rolls. Top with lettuce, tomatoes, pickles, and fried oysters. Serve with additional rémoulade.

CREOLE *Rémoulade*

Makes about 1 cup

³/₄ **CUP DUKE'S MAYONNAISE**

2 TABLESPOONS CHOPPED FRESH FLAT-LEAF PARSLEY

1 GREEN ONION, CHOPPED

1 CLOVE GARLIC, MINCED

2 TABLESPOONS CREOLE MUSTARD

1 TABLESPOON DRAINED CAPERS

Stir together all the ingredients in a medium bowl. Refrigerate until ready to serve or up to 2 days.

Bourride
(FISH STEW)
with AÏOLI

MAKES 4 TO 6 SERVINGS

~ ~

I am a Francophile and have been for quite a while. I spent the summer between my junior and senior years of college in Avignon, France, and was first introduced to this luscious stew then. The French love aïoli, and this dish celebrates it. As a friend remarked about this recipe, the soup is a vehicle for the aïoli toast. I couldn't agree more.

~ ~

	Aïoli (recipe follows)		
2	tablespoons olive oil	2	cups water
1	stalk celery, chopped	½	pound fingerling potatoes, halved lengthwise
1	fennel bulb, cored and sliced	2	pounds halibut (or other firm white fish such as cod or grouper)
1	large leek, thinly sliced	1	large egg yolk
1	large carrot, peeled and sliced		Dry sherry (optional)
1	(8-ounce) package sliced mushrooms		Chopped fresh flat-leaf parsley and fennel fronds
1½	cups dry white wine		Toasted baguette slices
1	(32-ounce) carton seafood stock		

Recipe Continues

1. Make the Aïoli. Refrigerate until ready to use.

2. Heat the oil in a Dutch oven or heavy stockpot over medium heat. Add the celery, fennel, leek, carrot, and mushrooms. Sauté for 10 minutes, or until the vegetables are very tender (but not browned). Add the wine and simmer until reduced by half. Stir in the stock and water and bring to a boil.

3. Add the potatoes and cook for 12 minutes, or until tender. Pour the mixture through a strainer over a large measuring cup or bowl. Set aside the vegetables and return the broth to the pot. Bring to a simmer.

4. Add the halibut to the simmering broth and poach for 5 to 6 minutes, until the fish flakes with a fork. Carefully remove the fish and divide evenly among serving bowls.

5. Whisk ½ cup of the Aïoli and the egg yolk in a medium bowl. Whisk in ¼ cup of the warm broth to temper. Stir the mixture into the broth in the pot. Cook for about 5 minutes or until slightly thickened (do not boil). Return the vegetables to the broth to warm. Stir in the sherry to taste, if desired.

6. To serve, pour the broth and vegetables evenly over the fish in the bowls. Garnish with fresh parsley and fennel fronds. Spread Aïoli onto the baguette slices and serve with the stew.

Aïoli

Makes about 1 cup

1 CUP DUKE'S MAYONNAISE

1¹⁄₂ TEASPOONS FRESH LEMON JUICE

1 TEASPOON DIJON MUSTARD

2 CLOVES GARLIC, MINCED

Stir together all the ingredients in a medium bowl. Refrigerate until ready to serve or up to 3 days.

When I moved to Oregon I knew some things would be different. Being on opposite coasts, I knew the weather, dress, and accents would all take some getting used to. But it didn't occur to me that Duke's Mayonnaise wouldn't exist there! Every year I look forward to having a turkey sandwich, post-Thanksgiving. It is turkey, salt and pepper, and Duke's on white bread. I was already upset about missing Thanksgiving with my family and then to find out there was no Duke's! I searched all over town. And of course I could not buy another brand. I told my mom, and she bought a case of Duke's and shipped it to me in Oregon. When quantities got low, she'd send another case. It's funny to note that I still have this problem when I visit my in-laws for Thanksgiving. They live in the Midwest so I have to bring my own Duke's.

—CHEF KEVIN GILLESPIE, RED BEARD
RESTAURANTS IN ATLANTA, GEORGIA

CHAPTER THREE

DINNER

Main Dishes

GRILLED ROSEMARY-DIJON

Pork Chops 97

Cottage Pie 103

HERB-ROASTED CHICKEN 124

SKILLET CHICKEN PARMESAN 98

GRILLED LAMB KEBAB WRAPS with Mint-Caper Sauce 109

TARRAGON CRAB CAKES
with Lemon-Shallot Tartar Sauce 119

CAST-IRON RIB EYES
with Mushrooms and Horseradish Sauce 100

Grilled Dry-Rub Chicken with White BBQ Sauce

112

Turkey Lettuce Wraps with Creamy Peanut Sauce 116

COCONUT-CRUSTED CHICKEN TENDERS
with Marmalade-Mustard Sauce 122

PECAN-CRUSTED FLOUNDER
with Lemon-Butter Cream Sauce 126

FIRECRACKER SHRIMP TACOS 129

PAPPARDELLE BOLOGNESE 137

MISO-GLAZED SALMON 106

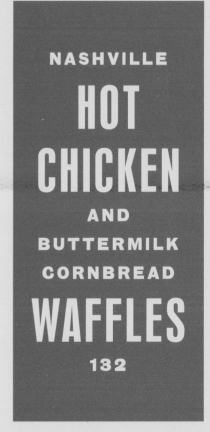

NASHVILLE HOT CHICKEN AND BUTTERMILK CORNBREAD WAFFLES 132

Grilled

ROSEMARY-DIJON

Pork Chops

MAKES 4 SERVINGS

This is such an easy main dish, perfect for those busy weeknights when you want something quick (and no dishes to clean up after). The only thing you've got to remember is to marinate the chops in the morning to have them ready to grill at dinnertime. I like to buy bone-in pork chops for extra flavor and moisture. If you're not in the mood for pork, this recipe is also great with chicken.

4	bone-in pork loin chops
½	cup Duke's Mayonnaise
¼	cup Dijon mustard
¼	cup dry white wine
2	tablespoons honey
2	tablespoons chopped fresh rosemary, plus more for garnish (optional)

1. Place the pork chops in a large zip-top plastic bag or shallow baking dish. Whisk together the mayonnaise, mustard, wine, honey, and rosemary. Pour over the pork chops, turn to coat, and seal the bag or cover the dish. Refrigerate for 8 hours or overnight.

2. Preheat the grill to medium-high heat. Remove the pork chops from the marinade, discarding the marinade. Grill the chops, covered with the grill lid, for 4 to 5 minutes on each side, until cooked through. Garnish with fresh rosemary, if desired.

Skillet
Chicken
PARMESAN

MAKES 4 SERVINGS

4	boneless, skinless chicken breasts (about 2 pounds)
¼	cup Duke's Mayonnaise
¼	teaspoon salt
¼	teaspoon freshly ground pepper
1	cup dry breadcrumbs
2	tablespoons all-purpose flour
1	tablespoon Italian seasoning
3	tablespoons vegetable oil
1	(24-ounce) jar marinara sauce
½	cup freshly grated Parmesan cheese
1	(8-ounce) ball fresh mozzarella, sliced
	Fresh basil leaves

This is the ultimate dinner to make when you want to impress your family. The best part about it is that it's so easy to put together (but no one has to know!). Serve with pasta and a green salad, and dinner is done.

1. Preheat the oven to 425°F.

2. Brush both sides of the chicken with the mayonnaise; sprinkle with the salt and pepper. Combine the breadcrumbs, flour, and Italian seasoning in a shallow dish. Dip the chicken in the breadcrumb mixture, pressing to coat evenly.

3. Heat the oil in a large cast-iron or other ovenproof skillet over medium-high heat. Brown the chicken for 2 to 3 minutes on each side. Remove from the heat. Pour the marinara sauce over the chicken, sprinkle with the Parmesan cheese, and arrange the mozzarella slices evenly over the top.

4. Transfer the skillet to the oven and bake at 425°F for 20 minutes, or until the chicken is cooked through and the cheese is melted and lightly browned. Top with basil leaves before serving.

TASTY TIP

Pound the chicken breasts to an equal thickness before coating so they cook evenly.

CAST-IRON
Rib Eyes

with MUSHROOMS AND HORSERADISH SAUCE

MAKES 4 SERVINGS

My cast-iron skillet is one of my favorite pieces of kitchen equipment. It's great for cooking just about anything, including steak. When Chris and I were dating and went on a camping trip with his buddies to the Florida Panhandle's Perdido Key, I was that girl who brought the cast-iron skillet along with a giant cooler. There may have been a few complaints initially, as I made the boys schlep my "outdoor kitchen" equipment about a mile across the beach to our campsite, but after a few campfire meals that didn't consist of beanie weanies I think they forgave me.

	Horseradish Sauce (recipe follows)
2	(1-pound) rib eye steaks (or use New York strip steaks)
	Kosher salt and freshly ground pepper
2	tablespoons olive oil
2	tablespoons salted butter
1	(16-ounce) package sliced fresh mushrooms

1. Prepare the Horseradish Sauce.

2. Sprinkle the steaks liberally with salt and pepper. Heat the oil and butter in a large cast-iron skillet over medium-high heat until hot. Add the steaks and cook for 4 to 5 minutes on each side, or to desired doneness, tilting the pan and basting the steaks with the melted butter mixture as they cook. Remove the steaks to a cutting board to rest for 10 minutes before slicing.

3. Add the mushrooms to the drippings in the skillet and cook for 6 to 8 minutes, until the mushrooms are browned and tender. Season with salt and pepper to taste.

4. To serve, divide the sliced steaks evenly between serving plates and top with the mushrooms. Serve with the Horseradish Sauce.

HORSERADISH Sauce

Makes about ¾ cup

½ CUP DUKE'S MAYONNAISE

3 TABLESPOONS SOUR CREAM

1 TABLESPOON PREPARED HORSERADISH

2 TEASPOONS DIJON MUSTARD

SALT AND FRESHLY GROUND PEPPER

Stir together all the ingredients in a medium bowl.
Refrigerate until ready to serve or up to 3 days.

Cottage Pie

MAKES 4 TO 6 SERVINGS

~ ~

This is the ultimate comforting one-dish dinner that I have mistakenly called shepherd's pie all my life. That was until our British friend Steve set me straight: Shepherd's pie is made with ground lamb (hence the shepherd), and cottage pie is made with ground beef. So where's the Duke's in this recipe? In the mashed potato topping. It makes the potatoes super creamy and fluffy.

~ ~

	Fluffy Mashed Potatoes (recipe follows)
1	tablespoon olive oil
1½	pounds ground beef
2	cloves garlic, minced
1	small onion, chopped
2	carrots, peeled and chopped
½	cup chopped celery
⅓	cup all-purpose flour
1	(14.5-ounce) can beef broth
½	cup dry red wine
2	tablespoons tomato paste
1	tablespoon Worcestershire sauce
1	cup frozen green peas, thawed
2	tablespoons salted butter, melted
	Chopped fresh flat-leaf parsley

1. Make the Fluffy Mashed Potatoes.

2. Preheat the oven to 350°F. Lightly grease 4 to 6 individual casseroles or a 2-quart baking dish.

3. Heat the oil in a large skillet or saucepan over medium-high heat. Add the ground beef and cook, breaking up the meat until it crumbles, for 5 minutes or until browned. Remove the beef from the skillet, reserving the drippings in the skillet.

4. Add the garlic, onion, carrots, and celery to the skillet. Cook for 5 minutes, or until the vegetables are tender. Sprinkle the flour over the vegetables and stir until combined (the mixture will be thick).

Recipe Continues

5. Stir together the broth, wine, tomato paste, and Worcestershire sauce. Add to the skillet and bring the mixture to a boil. Reduce the heat to medium-low and simmer for 5 minutes, or until the mixture thickens slightly. Return the beef to the skillet along with the peas and stir to combine.

6. Spoon the mixture into the prepared casseroles (or baking dish). Carefully top with the Fluffy Mashed Potatoes; scrape with a fork if desired to make a pretty pattern. Drizzle with the melted butter.

7. Bake the casseroles at 350°F for 30 minutes, or until bubbly. If desired, turn on the broiler and brown the mashed potato topping for 1 minute. Sprinkle with the parsley.

TASTY TIP

Let the beef filling cool before topping with the mashed potatoes to prevent them from sinking.

Fluffy
MASHED POTATOES

Makes 4 to 6 servings

3 POUNDS YUKON GOLD POTATOES, PEELED AND CUT INTO CHUNKS

$\frac{1}{2}$ CUP DUKE'S MAYONNAISE

$\frac{1}{3}$ CUP WHOLE MILK

$\frac{1}{4}$ CUP SALTED BUTTER

$\frac{1}{4}$ TEASPOON GROUND NUTMEG

SALT AND FRESHLY GROUND PEPPER

1. Bring the potatoes with salted water to cover to a boil in a large saucepot over medium-high heat. Boil for 15 minutes, or until the potatoes are tender. Drain and return to the pot.

2. Add the mayonnaise, milk, butter, and nutmeg to the potatoes. Mash with a potato masher or handheld mixer to desired consistency. Season with salt and pepper to taste.

The identity of Southern cooking is diversified and complex. Staple ingredients define and characterize the unique regions, from the rice crops of South Carolina to Louisiana cane syrup. One ingredient that stands out as a true point of pride throughout the South, crossing regional boundaries and state lines, is Duke's. With fervent fans and a cult-like chef following, it can easily be credited with being one of the defining flavors of the South. Among the first lessons I learned in Southern cooking is that no pantry is complete without Duke's Mayonnaise.

—WHITNEY OTAWKA, CHEF AND AUTHOR OF *THE SALTWATER TABLE*

Miso-Glazed
Salmon

MAKES 4 SERVINGS

Miso is an ingredient that I love. If you're unfamiliar with it, it's fermented soybean paste, and it adds the ever-desirable "umami" flavor to this dish. Mixed with mayonnaise, honey, and a little sriracha, it serves as a great glaze that browns up beautifully under the broiler. I choose a fattier salmon like Scottish salmon instead of coho. Serve with jasmine rice and steamed bok choy for an easy, elegant dinner in under 30 minutes.

1½	**pounds salmon fillets**
¼	**cup Duke's Mayonnaise**
4	**teaspoons white miso paste**
1	**tablespoon honey**
2	**teaspoons sriracha hot sauce**
2	**green onions, thinly sliced**

1. Preheat the oven to 450°F. Line a rimmed baking sheet with aluminum foil and lightly grease it. Place the salmon on the foil.

2. Stir together the mayonnaise, miso, honey, and sriracha in a small bowl. Brush half of the mixture all over the salmon fillets. Bake at 450°F for 8 minutes.

3. Turn on the broiler. Spoon the remaining sauce over the salmon. Broil for 1 to 2 minutes, until the sauce is browned and the salmon is cooked through. Sprinkle each serving with green onion.

TASTY TIP

Look for miso paste in the refrigerated or produce section at your grocery store.

It's usually sold in a tub and varies in flavor depending on the type you use. White miso is the mildest version and yields a sweet flavor. You may also use red miso in this recipe, but be aware that it's saltier than white miso so you may not need as much.

GRILLED
Lamb Kebab Wraps

with MINT-CAPER SAUCE

MAKES 4 SERVINGS

~ ~

I absolutely love Mediterranean food—the spices, fresh vegetables, grilled meats, and flatbread. These *kofta* (lamb meatballs), seasoned with fresh herbs, are kept juicy with the addition of Duke's. The kebabs are combined with crisp vegetables, slathered with creamy yogurt sauce, and surrounded by grilled naan for winning wraps sure to please. If you're not a fan of lamb, you may use ground beef or ground turkey instead.

~ ~

	Mint-Caper Sauce (recipe follows)	½	teaspoon ground coriander
1½	pounds ground lamb	¼	teaspoon salt
¼	cup dry breadcrumbs	¼	teaspoon freshly ground pepper
1½	tablespoons Duke's Mayonnaise	1	red onion, cut into wedges
1½	tablespoons chopped fresh mint	1	tablespoon olive oil
1½	tablespoons chopped fresh oregano	4	naan breads
1	teaspoon smoked paprika		Toppings: tomato wedges, thinly sliced cucumber, fresh mint

Recipe Continues

1. Preheat the grill to medium-high heat. Make the Mint-Caper Sauce.

2. Gently mix together the lamb, breadcrumbs, mayonnaise, mint, oregano, smoked paprika, and coriander in a medium bowl. Shape the mixture into 16 oval-shaped meatballs around metal skewers. Sprinkle with the salt and pepper.

3. Grill the kebabs, covered with the grill lid, for 6 to 8 minutes, turning occasionally, until cooked through. While the kebabs cook, brush the onion wedges with the olive oil and grill for 2 to 3 minutes on each side, until tender and grill marks appear.

4. Grill the naan breads for 30 seconds to 1 minute on each side, until warmed through.

5. To serve, spread desired amount of Mint-Caper Sauce on the naan breads. Top with the meatballs, tomato wedges, cucumbers, grilled onion, and fresh mint. Serve with additional sauce, if desired.

TASTY TIP

You can use 12-inch wooden skewers in place of metal ones. Just be sure to soak them in water for at least 30 minutes before grilling to prevent them from burning.

MINT-CAPER Sauce

Makes about 1½ cups

$3/4$ CUP DUKE'S MAYONNAISE

$1/2$ CUP PLAIN GREEK YOGURT

$1\frac{1}{2}$ TABLESPOONS CHOPPED FRESH MINT

$1\frac{1}{2}$ TABLESPOONS DRAINED CAPERS

$1\frac{1}{2}$ TABLESPOONS EXTRA-VIRGIN OLIVE OIL

$1\frac{1}{2}$ TEASPOONS GRATED LEMON ZEST

1 TABLESPOON FRESH LEMON JUICE

Stir together all the ingredients in a small bowl. Refrigerate until ready to serve or up to 2 days.

It is quite possible that the maddest my mother has been at me in recent years is when I was misquoted in an article about my affinity for Duke's. My exposure to Duke's was attributed to my childhood friend's mother. I actually used Mrs. Radford as the counterpoint of my love for Duke's because she religiously put Miracle Whip on all sandwiches at her house. My mother, a native of Richmond, was mortally offended. She knew she had raised me right!

Although we use a lot of Duke's in my restaurants, in my day-to-day eating life, I don't consume very much mayonnaise. The exception is during tomato season. Because of my long-standing devotion to eating seasonally, I have taken to referring to July and August as "Duke's Season."

—JOHN FLEER, EXECUTIVE CHEF/OWNER
OF RHUBARB, THE RHU, AND BENNE ON
EAGLE IN ASHEVILLE, NORTH CAROLINA

Grilled Dry-Rub Chicken

with WHITE BBQ SAUCE

MAKES 4 TO 6 SERVINGS

I was introduced to white barbecue sauce when I lived in Birmingham, Alabama, and frequented Saw's BBQ. The creamy and tangy sauce is perfect for drizzling on smoked or spice-rubbed chicken. This recipe calls for a cut-up chicken, and oftentimes you can buy it already cut up. Since they take the longest to cook, look for packages with smaller chicken breasts.

1	(4- to 5-pound) chicken, cut into drumsticks, thighs, breasts, and wings
1	tablespoon packed light brown sugar
1	tablespoon smoked paprika
1	tablespoon dried thyme
1	tablespoon dried oregano

1	teaspoon chili powder
1	teaspoon garlic powder
½	teaspoon salt
½	teaspoon freshly ground pepper
	White BBQ Sauce (recipe follows)

1. Place the chicken pieces in a large zip-top plastic bag or large shallow dish.

2. Stir together the brown sugar, smoked paprika, thyme, oregano, chili powder, garlic powder, salt, and pepper. Sprinkle the seasoning over the chicken pieces and toss to coat evenly. Seal the bag or cover the dish and refrigerate for 2 hours, tossing the chicken occasionally to season.

3. Let the chicken stand at room temperature for 30 minutes. While the chicken stands, make the White BBQ Sauce.

4. If using a charcoal grill, preheat one side of the grill to medium-high heat and the other side to medium heat. If using a gas grill, preheat the grill to medium-high.

5. Place the chicken over medium-high heat and sear for 2 to 3 minutes on each side. If using a charcoal grill, transfer the chicken to the side of the grill over medium heat. If using a gas grill, reduce the temperature to medium heat.

6. Grill, covered with the grill lid, for 15 to 40 minutes (depending on the cut of chicken), until a meat thermometer inserted into the thickest portion registers 170°F. (Wings take around 15 minutes, thighs and legs around 25 minutes, and chicken breasts 35 to 40 minutes.) Remove the chicken from the grill and let rest for 10 minutes before serving with White BBQ Sauce.

White BBQ SAUCE

Makes 1½ cups

1 CUP DUKE'S MAYONNAISE

3 TABLESPOONS WHITE VINEGAR

2 TABLESPOONS GRANULATED SUGAR

1 TABLESPOON PREPARED HORSERADISH

1 TEASPOON WORCESTERSHIRE SAUCE

1 TEASPOON FRESH LEMON JUICE

½ TEASPOON GARLIC POWDER

½ TEASPOON SALT

½ TEASPOON FRESHLY GROUND PEPPER

¼ TEASPOON CAYENNE PEPPER

Stir together all the ingredients in a medium bowl. Refrigerate until ready to serve or up to 3 days. (The flavors get better the longer the mixture stands.)

German
Potato Salad,
PAGE 155

White BBQ
Sauce,
PAGE 113

Confetti
Coleslaw,
PAGE 144

Grilled Dry-Rub Chicken, **PAGE 112**

Mom's Apple Pie, **PAGE 218**

TURKEY
Lettuce Wraps

with CREAMY PEANUT SAUCE

MAKES 4 SERVINGS

~ ~

Thailand was a bucket-list trip for me, and I was lucky enough to go there in the fall of 2013. Our first stop was Railay Beach on Krabi province, where we took a long-tail boat from the mainland and rode up as close to shore as we could. We rolled up our pant legs and hopped out of the boat to wade to shore with our luggage lifted high on our shoulders. Besides the sugary sand beaches, crystal aqua blue water, and a naughty monkey stealing a coconut right out of a child's hands, the most memorable part of the trip was the food. There were flavors I had never experienced before. We were there when the weather was hot; a meal of crisp lettuce filled with flavorful meat and vegetables and topped with a savory peanut sauce was a welcome treat. Here is my take on the lettuce wraps we enjoyed on our trip.

~ ~

	Creamy Peanut Sauce (recipe follows)
1	tablespoon dark sesame oil
1½	pounds ground turkey
3	cloves garlic, minced
1	tablespoon minced fresh ginger
1	tablespoon vegetable oil
1	(5-ounce) package sliced shiitake mushrooms
1	(8-ounce) can diced water chestnuts, drained and minced

⅓	cup hoisin sauce
1½	teaspoons fish sauce
1	large head Bibb or butter lettuce, leaves separated
1	cup matchstick-cut carrots
1	red chile pepper, sliced (optional)
	Fresh cilantro leaves
	Fresh basil leaves
	Chopped salted roasted peanuts

Recipe Continues

1. Make the Creamy Peanut Sauce.

2. Heat the sesame oil in a large skillet over medium-high heat. Add the turkey, garlic, and ginger and sauté for 5 minutes, or until the turkey is browned. Remove the turkey from the skillet.

3. Add the vegetable oil to the drippings in the skillet and heat over medium-high heat until hot. Add the mushrooms and sauté for 5 minutes, or until the mushrooms are browned and tender. Remove the skillet from the heat and stir the turkey mixture and water chestnuts into the mushrooms.

4. Stir together the hoisin sauce and fish sauce. Add to the turkey mixture and stir to combine. Place the skillet over medium heat and cook for 2 minutes, or until the mixture is hot.

5. To serve, divide the turkey mixture evenly among the lettuce leaves. Top with the carrots, sliced chile, if using, cilantro, basil, and chopped peanuts. Drizzle with the Creamy Peanut Sauce and serve immediately.

Creamy PEANUT SAUCE

Makes about ²/₃ cup

3 TABLESPOONS CREAMY PEANUT BUTTER

3 TABLESPOONS DUKE'S MAYONNAISE

2 TABLESPOONS REDUCED-SODIUM SOY SAUCE

1 TABLESPOON FRESH LIME JUICE

2 TEASPOONS LIGHT BROWN SUGAR

2 TEASPOONS ASIAN CHILE-GARLIC PASTE (SUCH AS SAMBAL OELEK)

1 TEASPOON GRATED FRESH GINGER

Stir together all the ingredients in a small bowl. Refrigerate until ready to serve or up to 2 days.

TASTY TIP
Use a Microplane to easily grate the ginger.

TARRAGON
Crab Cakes

with LEMON-SHALLOT TARTAR SAUCE

MAKES 4 SERVINGS

I grew up on Isle of Hope, Georgia, on the best street. My best friend (who still is to this day) lived across the street, and when we weren't playing together, I was likely at my grandparents' house. Many weekends and summer days were spent at Mema and Dado's. They lived a bike ride away on a tidal creek, so my sister, cousins, and I would spend many afternoons there swimming, crabbing, and throwing a cast net off the dock. Sure, we could pull the crab trap up and catch crab that way, but our preferred method was holding a line in the water attached to a chicken neck and a basket, patiently awaiting that little tickle from a crab on the end. Nowadays, since I don't have the time to cook and clean the crab, I buy it from the local seafood market. Lump crabmeat tends to have fewer pieces of shell and cartilage and is a gorgeous bright white color.

	Lemon-Shallot Tartar Sauce (recipe follows)
1	pound lump crabmeat
1½	cups fresh breadcrumbs
½	cup Duke's Mayonnaise
¼	cup chopped fresh flat-leaf parsley
2	tablespoons chopped fresh tarragon

1	teaspoon grated lemon zest
½	teaspoon paprika
1	tablespoon olive oil
	Salt and freshly ground pepper
	Lemon wedges
	Fresh flat-leaf parsley, fresh tarragon, and/or watercress (optional)

Recipe Continues

1. Make the Lemon-Shallot Tartar Sauce.

2. Gently pick through the crabmeat to remove any shell or cartilage. Place in a medium bowl with the breadcrumbs.

3. Stir together the mayonnaise, parsley, tarragon, lemon zest, and paprika. Pour over the crabmeat mixture and toss gently to combine. Shape the mixture into 8 patties.

4. Heat the oil in a large nonstick skillet over medium-high heat. Cook the crab cakes for 2 to 3 minutes on each side, until browned and heated through. Sprinkle with salt and pepper to taste. Serve with lemon wedges and Lemon-Shallot Tartar Sauce. Garnish, if desired.

TASTY TIP

Backfin and claw crabmeat are not as pretty as lump, but they're often cheaper and just as flavorful, and will work great in this recipe, too.

LEMON-SHALLOT Tartar Sauce

Makes about ¾ cup

½ CUP DUKE'S MAYONNAISE

2 TABLESPOONS MINCED DILL PICKLES

1 TABLESPOON MINCED SHALLOT

1 TABLESPOON SOUR CREAM

1 TABLESPOON FRESH LEMON JUICE

Stir together all the ingredients in a small bowl. Refrigerate until ready to serve or up to 2 days.

COCONUT-CRUSTED Chicken Tenders

with MARMALADE-MUSTARD SAUCE

MAKES 4 TO 6 SERVINGS

½	cup all-purpose flour
2	large eggs
1	tablespoon water
2½	cups sweetened flaked coconut
2	pounds chicken tenders
¼	cup Duke's Mayonnaise
	Salt and freshly ground pepper
	Marmalade-Mustard Sauce (recipe follows)

Let's be honest: These are grown-ups' chicken fingers with a fancy, yet easy, mustard sauce (although my child loves them too). The Duke's acts as a binder and seals in the juiciness of the chicken as it cooks. That's another thing: The tenders are baked in the oven instead of deep-fried, so you can enjoy them guilt-free. It's easy to close your eyes as you taste the sweet, nutty coconut and tangy orange-mustard sauce and imagine yourself sitting on the beach somewhere in the Caribbean.

1. Preheat the oven to 400°F. Line a rimmed baking sheet with aluminum foil, place a wire rack on top of the foil, and coat the rack with cooking spray.

2. Place the flour in a shallow dish or plate. Whisk together the eggs and water in a separate shallow dish. Place the coconut in another separate shallow dish.

3. Arrange the chicken tenders in a single layer on a plate or baking sheet. Brush one side of each tender with half of the mayonnaise. Dip the mayonnaise-coated sides in the flour and return the chicken, coated sides down, to the plate. Brush the other sides with the remaining mayonnaise and dip in the flour.

4. Dredge both sides in the egg mixture, and then in the coconut, pressing to adhere. Place the chicken tenders on the wire rack in the baking sheet.

5. Bake the tenders at 400°F for 20 to 25 minutes, until the chicken is cooked through and the coconut is lightly browned. Sprinkle with salt and pepper to taste.

6. While the tenders are baking, make the Marmalade-Mustard Sauce and serve with the hot tenders.

Marmalade— MUSTARD SAUCE

Makes about 1 cup

¾ CUP DUKE'S MAYONNAISE

3 TABLESPOONS ORANGE MARMALADE

1½ TEASPOONS YELLOW MUSTARD

¼ TEASPOON PAPRIKA

Stir together all the ingredients in a small bowl.
Refrigerate until ready to serve or up to 5 days.

Herb-Roasted
Chicken

MAKES 4 SERVINGS

Of all the recipes to master, everyone should know how to roast a chicken. This one couldn't be easier, and it comes out browned and juicy and is so much better than a store-bought rotisserie chicken. For the best results, be sure to create an even base with the onions, garlic, and lemon. The chicken sits atop and absorbs the aromatics as it roasts, and the mayonnaise sauce locks in the moisture for great results every time.

1	(4- to 5-pound) roasting chicken
1	teaspoon kosher salt
1	teaspoon freshly ground pepper
2	heads garlic, cut in half crosswise
2	lemons, halved
1	(1-ounce) package fresh sage, plus more for garnish (optional)
¼	cup fresh flat-leaf parsley leaves, plus more for garnish (optional)
2	sweet onions, peeled, trimmed, and cut in half crosswise
1	red onion, peeled, trimmed, and cut in half crosswise
½	cup Duke's Mayonnaise
1	tablespoon fresh lemon juice
1	teaspoon Worcestershire sauce
½	teaspoon reduced-sodium soy sauce

1. Sprinkle the chicken, inside and out, with the salt and pepper and let stand for 1 hour in the refrigerator.

2. Preheat the oven to 425°F. Place 1 halved head garlic, 1 halved lemon, and half of the sage and parsley inside the chicken cavity.

3. Arrange the onions, remaining garlic, remaining lemon, and remaining herbs in the bottom of a roasting pan to create a base for the chicken.

4. Stir together the mayonnaise, lemon juice, Worcestershire sauce, and soy sauce. Carefully loosen the skin away from the chicken breasts and thighs. Spoon about half of the mayonnaise mixture in between the skin and meat. Massage the mixture into the chicken. Tie the chicken legs with kitchen twine; pull the wing tips up and back behind the wing drumettes.

5. Place the chicken on top of the onions, garlic, and lemon. Brush the chicken all over with the remaining mayonnaise mixture.

6. Bake the chicken at 425°F for 55 to 65 minutes, until a thermometer inserted in the thickest part of the thigh registers 170°F. Let rest for 10 minutes before slicing. Garnish with additional fresh herbs if desired.

Pecan-Crusted
Flounder
with LEMON-BUTTER CREAM SAUCE

MAKES 4 SERVINGS

To this day, one of my favorite restaurants is the Last Resort Grill in Athens, Georgia. Maybe it's because it reminds me of college date-night dinners before a sorority function, or maybe it's that their food is just so good. I dream about the pecan-crusted fish on their menu, and since it's harder to get back to Athens now that I have a family, here's my take on that dish.

	Lemon-Butter Cream Sauce (recipe follows)
1½	cups chopped pecans
½	cup dry breadcrumbs
2	teaspoons grated lemon zest
1½	pounds skinless flounder fillets (or use trout or other flaky white fish)
¼	cup Duke's Mayonnaise
½	teaspoon salt
½	teaspoon freshly ground pepper
4	tablespoons olive oil, divided

1. Make the Lemon-Butter Cream Sauce. Keep warm.

2. Pulse the pecans, breadcrumbs, and lemon zest in a food processor until very finely chopped. Place the mixture in a shallow pan or dish.

3. Brush one side of the fish fillets with half of the mayonnaise. Sprinkle with ¼ teaspoon each salt and pepper. Dredge the coated sides of the fish in the pecan mixture; brush the remaining sides with the remaining mayonnaise and sprinkle with the remaining salt and pepper. Dredge in the remaining pecan mixture.

4. Heat 2 tablespoons of the oil in a large nonstick skillet over medium-high heat. Cook half of the fish fillets for 2 to 3 minutes on each side, until the fish flakes with a fork. Carefully remove the fish to serving plates. Repeat with the remaining oil and fish. Serve the fish with the Lemon-Butter Cream Sauce.

LEMON-BUTTER
Cream Sauce

Makes about ⅔ cup

¼ CUP SALTED BUTTER

1 CLOVE GARLIC, MINCED

1 TEASPOON DIJON MUSTARD

1½ TABLESPOONS FRESH
LEMON JUICE

1 CUP HEAVY CREAM

SALT AND FRESHLY GROUND
PEPPER

1. Melt the butter in a small saucepan over medium heat. Add the garlic and cook for 1 minute, until tender.

2. Whisk in the mustard, lemon juice, and cream. Carefully bring to a simmer. (Watch the pan so the mixture doesn't boil over.) Simmer for 6 to 8 minutes, until the sauce is reduced and thickened. Season with salt and pepper to taste.

Firecracker
Shrimp Tacos

MAKES 4 TO 6 SERVINGS

~ ~

These beer-battered Baja-style tacos are topped with a cilantro-lime slaw and a drizzle of sweet and spicy firecracker sauce. They are sure to be a hit for Taco Tuesday—or any day of the week! To save time, buy already peeled and deveined shrimp. Or, buy about 1½ pounds medium shrimp to get the 1¼ pounds peeled and deveined you need for the recipe. I recommend making the slaw first to allow the dressing to soften the cabbage while the shrimp cooks.

~ ~

	Firecracker Sauce (recipe follows)
	Cilantro-Lime Slaw (recipe follows)
	Vegetable or peanut oil, for frying
1½	**cups all-purpose flour**
1	**teaspoon garlic powder**
1	**teaspoon paprika**
½	**teaspoon baking powder**

¼	**teaspoon salt**
¼	**teaspoon freshly ground pepper**
1½	**cups lager beer**
1¼	**pounds peeled and deveined medium shrimp**
2	**avocados, pitted, peeled, and sliced**
12	**corn tortillas, charred or warmed**
	Lime wedges

Recipe Continues

1. Make the Firecracker Sauce and the Cilantro-Lime Slaw.

2. Pour oil to a depth of 3 inches into a Dutch oven or other large heavy pot. Heat to 375°F over medium-high heat. Line a large baking sheet with paper towels.

3. While the oil heats, combine the flour, garlic powder, paprika, baking powder, salt, and pepper in a medium bowl. Add the beer and whisk until smooth.

4. Dip the shrimp, one at a time, in the batter and turn until completely coated. In batches, add the coated shrimp to the hot oil and fry, turning occasionally, for 2 to 3 minutes, until browned and cooked through. Drain the shrimp on the paper towels.

5. To serve, divide the Cilantro-Lime Slaw, shrimp, and avocado slices evenly among the tortillas. Drizzle with the Firecracker Sauce and serve with lime wedges.

TASTY TIP

For added flavor, I like to char the corn tortillas over a gas burner or on the grill.

Firecracker SAUCE

Makes about ½ cup

½ CUP DUKE'S MAYONNAISE

1 TABLESPOON SWEET CHILI SAUCE

1 TEASPOON SRIRACHA HOT SAUCE

1 TEASPOON HONEY

Stir together the mayonnaise, chili sauce, sriracha, and honey in a small bowl. Refrigerate until ready to serve or up to 5 days.

CILANTRO-LIME Slaw

Makes about 4 cups

1 TEASPOON GRATED LIME ZEST

1 TABLESPOON FRESH LIME JUICE

1 TABLESPOON OLIVE OIL

1 TABLESPOON HONEY

$1/4$ TEASPOON SALT

$1/4$ TEASPOON FRESHLY GROUND PEPPER

2 CUPS SLICED RED CABBAGE

2 CUPS SLICED GREEN CABBAGE

$1/2$ CUP COARSELY CHOPPED FRESH CILANTRO

Stir together the lime zest, lime juice, oil, honey, salt, and pepper in a medium bowl. Add the cabbage and cilantro leaves and toss to coat. Let stand while cooking the shrimp.

Nashville
Hot
Chicken

AND BUTTERMILK CORNBREAD WAFFLES

MAKES 8 SERVINGS

~ ~

I have a confession: When I first heard of the chicken-and-waffle trend I didn't get it. It seemed like such an odd combination. But then I tried it on a trip visiting Chris's Aunt Laura and Uncle Don in Nashville and was hooked. What is there not to love about an excuse to have breakfast for dinner? My version combines *very* spicy Nashville hot chicken with savory cornbread waffles. A shower of sweet maple syrup helps tame the flames from the chicken, but dial back the amount of cayenne pepper in the hot oil if you're sensitive to spice. Duke's plays two important roles in this recipe: It acts as a tenderizer in the chicken's buttermilk marinade, and it makes the waffles fluffy and moist. When making the chicken, please don't skip the step of letting the chicken come to room temperature before breading and frying. If you do, you'll either end up with very dark skin by the time the insides are cooked, or you'll get perfectly browned and crispy skin but underdone meat.

~ ~

Recipe Continues

3	cups whole buttermilk
½	cup Duke's Mayonnaise
¼	cup dill pickle juice
8	skin-on, bone-in chicken thighs
8	chicken legs
	Buttermilk Cornbread Waffles (recipe follows)
	Peanut oil, for frying
2	cups self-rising flour
	Salt
3	tablespoons cayenne pepper
1	tablespoon packed brown sugar
1	teaspoon garlic powder
1	teaspoon paprika
½	teaspoon chili powder
	Maple syrup

1. Whisk together the buttermilk, mayonnaise, and pickle juice. Combine with the chicken in an extra-large zip-top plastic bag. Seal and chill overnight.

2. Remove the chicken from the marinade, and discard the marinade. Let the chicken stand at room temperature for 1 hour.

3. While the chicken stands, make the Buttermilk Cornbread Waffles. Keep warm in a low oven while you fry the chicken.

4. Pour oil to a depth of 3 inches in a large Dutch oven over medium-high heat. Heat to 325°F. Dredge the chicken in the flour, shaking off the excess. Fry the chicken, in batches, for 12 to 15 minutes, until the chicken reaches 170°F. Drain on a wire rack, then sprinkle with salt to taste. When the frying oil is cool, reserve 1 cup and set aside.

5. Carefully whisk together the reserved frying oil, the cayenne pepper, brown sugar, garlic powder, paprika, and chili powder. Brush desired amount over the chicken.

6. To serve, top each waffle with chicken, and drizzle with maple syrup.

TASTY TIP

The pickle juice in the marinade adds crucial tangy flavor that the chicken absorbs.

If you're looking for a recipe that uses the pickles, try Mile-High Bacon Cheeseburgers with Burger Sauce (page 79) or Oyster Po' Boys with Creole Rémoulade (page 86).

Buttermilk
CORNBREAD WAFFLES

Makes 8 waffles

2 CUPS SELF-RISING YELLOW CORNMEAL MIX

2 TABLESPOONS GRANULATED SUGAR

1/4 TEASPOON SALT

1 CUP WHOLE BUTTERMILK

1/2 CUP DUKE'S MAYONNAISE

1/4 CUP VEGETABLE OIL

1 LARGE EGG

1. Preheat a waffle iron according to manufacturer's instructions.

2. Whisk together the cornmeal mix, sugar, and salt in a large bowl. Whisk together the buttermilk, mayonnaise, oil, and egg in a separate bowl. Add the buttermilk mixture to the cornmeal mixture, whisking until smooth.

3. Coat the waffle iron with cooking spray. Spoon the batter onto the hot waffle iron and cook according to manufacturer's instructions.

TASTY TIPS

Waffle irons typically have four wells, so you'll need to cook the waffles in two batches.

The waffle batter has self-rising cornmeal mix, so don't be surprised when the second batch of batter fluffs up as it stands.

For a sweeter waffle, increase the sugar to 3 tablespoons.

Pappardelle
Bolognese

MAKES 4 SERVINGS

This dish is inspired by my Mimi's Bolognese, a recipe she began making after our family traveled to Italy together and stayed in homes in Tuscany. The sauce is a labor of love, as it takes several hours of simmering to get it just right. After one taste, though, you'll realize it's worth it. I always knew I was in for a treat when I'd walk into Mimi's house and get a whiff of this luscious sauce. We'd often make crespelles with it, Italy's version of crêpes, but I really like it with pappardelle pasta.

1	tablespoon olive oil
3	tablespoons salted butter
1	cup diced onion
½	cup chopped celery
½	cup chopped carrots
½	pound ground chuck
½	pound ground mild pork sausage
1	cup whole milk
¼	teaspoon grated nutmeg
½	teaspoon salt
½	teaspoon freshly ground pepper
1	cup dry white wine
1	(28-ounce) can whole plum tomatoes, undrained and chopped
	Pappardelle Pasta (recipe follows)
	Freshly grated Parmesan cheese
	Basil leaves (optional)

1. Heat the oil and butter in a Dutch oven or large heavy saucepan over medium-high heat. Add the onion, celery, and carrots and sauté for 5 minutes, or until the vegetables are tender.

2. Add the ground chuck and sausage and cook, breaking up the meat until it crumbles, for 5 minutes, until browned.

3. Add the milk and simmer for 8 minutes, until the milk is evaporated. Stir in the nutmeg, salt, and pepper. Add the wine and simmer until the wine is evaporated. Add the tomatoes and bring to a boil. Reduce the heat to low and simmer, uncovered, for 3 hours, stirring occasionally. If the sauce becomes too dry, add water, ½ cup at a time.

4. While the sauce simmers, make the Pappardelle Pasta.

5. Either toss the hot pasta (and a few tablespoons pasta water) with the hot Bolognese sauce, or divide the pasta evenly among serving bowls and top with the sauce. Sprinkle each serving with Parmesan cheese and garnish with basil leaves, if desired.

Recipe Continues

PAPPARDELLE
Pasta

**Makes 14 ounces
(about 4 servings)**

2 CUPS ALL-PURPOSE FLOUR

¼ TEASPOON SALT

2 LARGE EGGS

3 TABLESPOONS DUKE'S
MAYONNAISE

1 TO 2 TABLESPOONS WATER

1. Pulse the flour and salt in a food processor to combine. Add the eggs and mayonnaise and pulse until blended. With the motor running, add 1 tablespoon water through the food chute and process until a dough forms. Add an additional 1 tablespoon water if needed. Turn out the dough onto a lightly floured surface and knead for about 10 minutes, or until the dough is firm, smooth, and elastic. Cover and let the dough rest for 1 hour.

2. Cut the dough into four equal portions. Cover three portions. To roll out the dough, follow the method for either a pasta machine or for using a rolling pin.

If using a pasta attachment or pasta machine

1. Flatten one dough portion (to facilitate passing in through the roller). Dust the dough with flour and pass it through the number one setting of the pasta roller twice. Fold the dough into thirds and pass it through the number one setting again.

2. Change the setting on the machine to number two and pass the dough through the roller. Continue to roll the pasta through the machine, increasing the setting each time to a larger number up to number five. Arrange the pasta dough sheet on a lightly floured surface while you repeat the process with the remaining dough pieces.

3. Carefully stack the dough sheets on top of each other and fold both ends of the stack over each other until they meet in the middle. Use a sharp knife to cut the dough into 1-inch-wide strips. Separate the noodles and let "dry" on a lightly floured surface while bringing the water for the pasta to a boil.

4. Bring a large pot of salted water to a boil. Add the noodles and cook for 3 minutes, or until al dente. Drain the noodles, reserving some of the pasta water, and serve hot with the Bolognese sauce.

If using a rolling pin

1. Flatten one dough portion. Dust the dough with flour and place on a lightly floured surface. Roll the dough into a thin 3- to 4-inch-wide strip. Fold the dough into thirds and roll out again.

2. Roll the dough as thinly as possible, but still thick enough to be lifted off the counter without breaking. (The dough should be paper thin, but you shouldn't be able to see through it.) Repeat the process with the remaining dough pieces.

3. Carefully stack the dough sheets on top of each other and fold both ends of the stack over each other until they meet in the middle. Use a sharp knife to cut the dough into 1-inch-wide strips. Separate the noodles and let "dry" on a lightly floured surface while bringing the water for the pasta to a boil.

4. Bring a large pot of salted water to a boil. Add the noodles and cook for 3 minutes, or until al dente. Drain the noodles, reserving some of the water, and serve hot with the Bolognese sauce.

CHAPTER FOUR

SIDES and SNACKS

Deviled Eggs
THREE WAYS 145

Confetti Coleslaw 144

SWEET POTATO AU GRATIN 163

NEW-SCHOOL WALDORF SALAD 149

ELOTE (GRILLED MEXICAN STREET CORN) 156

GRILLED OKRA
with Tomato Aïoli 153

Rosemary French Fries with Aïoli
170

Tostones with Cilantro-Jalapeño Green Sauce 167

FRIED BRUSSELS SPROUTS
WITH CREAMY HONEY-BALSAMIC DRIZZLE 160

GERMAN POTATO SALAD
WITH WARM BACON VINAIGRETTE 155

SMOKED GOUDA, CHEDDAR, AND PARMESAN

MAC 'N' CHEESE
150

LOADED TWICE-BAKED POTATOES 159

CORN AND BASIL HUSH PUPPIES 165

SHOWN ON PAGE 114

Confetti
Coleslaw

MAKES 8 TO 10 SERVINGS

~ ~

This coleslaw is just as much a feast for the eyes as it is for the stomach. The rainbow of shredded vegetables will add beauty to any feast. The recipe makes a lot, so it's perfect for serving a crowd at picnics or as a topping for tacos at a taco party. The slaw gets better as it stands in the fridge and the flavors develop, so it's also a great make-ahead side dish.

~ ~

3	cups shredded red cabbage
3	cups shredded green cabbage
1	red bell pepper, thinly sliced
1	yellow bell pepper, thinly sliced
4	carrots, shredded (2 cups)
2	green onions, sliced
½	cup chopped fresh flat-leaf parsley
⅓	cup Duke's Mayonnaise
¼	cup sugar
1	tablespoon white vinegar
1	tablespoon Dijon mustard
1	tablespoon olive oil
½	teaspoon salt
½	teaspoon freshly ground pepper

1. Combine the cabbages, bell peppers, carrots, green onions, and parsley in a large bowl.

2. Whisk together the mayonnaise, sugar, vinegar, mustard, olive oil, salt, and pepper in a small bowl. Pour the dressing over the cabbage mixture and toss to coat. Cover and let stand at least 30 minutes before serving to allow the vegetables to soften.

TASTY TIP

Use a box grater to shred the carrots.

Deviled Eggs

THREE WAYS

MAKES 1 DOZEN DEVILED EGGS

There's a good chance that you'll find deviled eggs at any Southern get-together—whether for Easter, a baby shower, or even a casual weekend brunch. What you won't find in my deviled eggs are pickles. I'm a purist when it comes to these little babies, and as far as I'm concerned pickles have no place in deviled eggs. So what I provide is traditional (no-pickle) deviled eggs, plus two (no-pickle) ways to jazz them up: If you want a little spice, try the Smoky Chipotle-Cilantro, or if you're a BLT fan, try the Pesto-Tomato-Bacon. Or, for a fun presentation, try all three.

1	dozen large eggs
1	teaspoon baking soda
1/3	cup Duke's Mayonnaise
2	teaspoons yellow mustard
1/2	teaspoon white vinegar
	Salt and freshly ground pepper

1. Place the eggs in a medium saucepan of cold water to cover. Add the baking soda and bring the water to a boil over high heat. Once boiling, remove the pan from the heat and cover the pan. Let stand for 12 minutes.

2. Fill a bowl with ice and water. Drain the eggs and plunge in the ice water bath. Let stand until cool.

3. Peel the eggs and cut in half lengthwise. Scoop out the cooked yolk into a bowl, reserving the whites.

4. Mash the egg yolks with a fork until finely crumbled. Stir in the mayonnaise, mustard, and vinegar. Season with salt and pepper to taste.

5. Spoon or pipe the filling into the egg whites. Cover and refrigerate until ready to serve or up to 2 days.

Recipe Continues

Smoky Chipotle-Cilantro Deviled Eggs

Prepare the Deviled Eggs through step 4, omitting the vinegar. Stir 1 tablespoon minced chipotle pepper in adobo sauce (from a 7-ounce can) and 2 teaspoons of the adobo sauce into the yolk mixture. Spoon or pipe the filling into the egg whites. Garnish the deviled eggs with cilantro leaves.

Pesto-Tomato-Bacon Deviled Eggs

Prepare the Deviled Eggs as directed, then spoon ½ teaspoon jarred pesto onto each filled egg half and top with a slice of cherry tomato and some crumbled bacon.

TASTY TIPS

A little baking soda is my secret for making the eggs easier to peel.

You can also buy already peeled eggs if you're short on time (or don't want the hassle). To easily fill the egg whites, I like to pipe the filling with a zip-top bag: Spoon the creamy egg yolk filling into a large bag, snip the corner, and squeeze the filling into the egg whites.

NEW-SCHOOL
Waldorf Salad

MAKES 10 TO 12 SERVINGS

I have always loved the flavors of Waldorf salad, but some versions I've had seem to have more dressing than apples. In my version, I've added endive, a lettuce with slight bitterness, to complement the sweet apples and dressing. If you aren't a fan of endive or frisée, feel free to substitute romaine, green leaf lettuce, or peppery arugula.

1	Pink Lady or other sweet red apple, halved, cored, and very thinly sliced
1	Granny Smith apple, halved, cored, and very thinly sliced
½	cup chopped walnuts, toasted
1	head curly endive or frisée lettuce, chopped
1	cup thinly sliced celery
1	cup halved red grapes
½	cup coarsely chopped fresh flat-leaf parsley
½	cup Duke's Mayonnaise
2	tablespoons plain yogurt
1	tablespoon apple cider vinegar
1	tablespoon honey
1	tablespoon extra-virgin olive oil
¼	teaspoon salt
¼	teaspoon freshly ground pepper

1. Combine the apples, walnuts, lettuce, celery, grapes, and parsley in a large serving bowl.

2. Whisk together the mayonnaise, yogurt, vinegar, honey, oil, salt, and pepper in a small bowl. Pour the dressing over the salad and toss, or serve the dressing on the side.

TASTY TIP

Want to make this salad ahead? Toss the apples with a little lemon water or seltzer to prevent them from browning.

SMOKED GOUDA, CHEDDAR, *and* PARMESAN
Mac 'n' Cheese

MAKES 6 SERVINGS

This home-run dish will please the whole family—from little kids to kids at heart. Experiment with your favorite cheeses, but I recommend keeping the Gouda. It lends the crucial smoky flavor to the pasta that makes this mac and cheese special. Bake and serve in a 2-quart baking dish or in individual dishes.

1	(16-ounce) package corkscrew pasta
1	(8-ounce) package smoked Gouda cheese, shredded
1	(8-ounce) block extra-sharp Cheddar cheese, shredded
4	ounces freshly grated Parmesan cheese
1½	cups Duke's Mayonnaise
1	cup sour cream
¼	teaspoon cayenne pepper
¼	teaspoon ground nutmeg
¼	teaspoon salt
1	cup fresh breadcrumbs
¼	cup salted butter, melted

1. Preheat the oven to 325°F. Cook the pasta in boiling salted water according to package directions until al dente. Drain and transfer to a large bowl.

2. Stir in the cheeses, mayonnaise, sour cream, cayenne pepper, nutmeg, and salt. Spoon into 6 lightly greased individual baking dishes or a 2-quart baking dish.

3. Stir together the breadcrumbs and melted butter. Sprinkle over the top. Bake the pasta at 325°F for 30 minutes, or until the topping is browned and the mixture is bubbly.

TASTY TIP

To make fresh breadcrumbs, pulse a few pieces of (preferably stale) bread in a food processor until crumbly.

Grilled Okra

with TOMATO AÏOLI

MAKES 4 SERVINGS

~ ~

So many people are afraid of okra because of the "slime" factor. But grilling them prevents slime from happening. Here, they are paired with their match made in heaven—tomatoes—in the form of tomato aïoli. Word to the wise: Small okra pods are more tender than large ones.

~ ~

	Tomato Aïoli (recipe follows)
1½	pounds okra pods, halved lengthwise
1	tablespoon olive oil
¼	teaspoon salt
¼	teaspoon freshly ground pepper

1. Preheat the grill to medium-high heat. Make the Tomato Aïoli while the grill heats.

2. Toss together the okra, oil, salt, and pepper. Place the okra in a grill basket and grill over medium-high heat for 4 to 6 minutes, turning occasionally, until tender. (If you don't have a grill basket, you can thread the okra onto double skewers, if desired, to help prevent them from falling between the grates.)

3. Remove the okra to a platter and serve hot with the Tomato Aïoli.

TASTY TIP

If the weather is not ideal, you can also use a grill pan or hot cast-iron skillet to cook the okra indoors.

Recipe Continues

Tomato AÏOLI

Makes ¾ cup

½ CUP DUKE'S MAYONNAISE

¼ CUP DRAINED SUN-DRIED TOMATOES IN OIL

2 TABLESPOONS WATER

2 TEASPOONS WHITE WINE VINEGAR

2 TEASPOONS OLIVE OIL

1½ TEASPOONS TOMATO PASTE

½ TEASPOON GARLIC POWDER

Puree all the ingredients in a food processor or blender until combined. Refrigerate until ready to serve or up to 2 days.

SHOWN ON PAGE 114

GERMAN
Potato Salad

with WARM BACON VINAIGRETTE

MAKES 8 TO 10 SERVINGS

3	pounds baby yellow and red potatoes
8	slices bacon
1	cup chopped onion
¼	cup Duke's Mayonnaise
2	tablespoons apple cider vinegar
2	tablespoons whole-grain mustard
1	tablespoon Dijon mustard
¼	teaspoon salt
¼	teaspoon freshly ground pepper
¼	cup chopped fresh flat-leaf parsley

Potato salad with a creamy and tangy *bacon* vinaigrette? I'm sold. While traditional German potato salad has only vinegar and mustard, I like to add a little Duke's to the mix to mellow it out (and prevent the backs of my cheeks from puckering).

1. Bring the potatoes and salted water to cover to a boil over medium-high heat. Cook for 15 minutes, or until tender. Drain and cool completely. Once cool, cut the potatoes into quarters and place in a serving bowl.

2. Cook the bacon in a large skillet over medium-high heat for 6 to 8 minutes, until crisp. Drain the bacon on paper towels, reserving 3 tablespoons drippings in the skillet.

3. Add the onion to the drippings in the skillet and cook for 6 minutes, or until tender. Remove the skillet from the heat. Stir together the mayonnaise, vinegar, mustards, salt, and pepper and add to the onion and drippings.

4. Crumble the bacon. Pour the dressing over the potatoes. Add the bacon and parsley and toss to coat. Serve warm or at room temperature.

TASTY TIP

Have you ever made potato salad that turned into mush once you mixed it together? The trick is to wait until the potatoes are completely cool before cutting them into quarters.

Elote

(GRILLED MEXICAN STREET CORN)

MAKES 8 SERVINGS

~ ~

I first had this dish at Café Habana in New York City when I was attending culinary school, and it was life-changing. It takes grilled corn to the next level by brushing the ears with creamy mayonnaise, rolling them in fluffy cheese, and then sprinkling with warm spices. If you can't find pretty corn with husks, use corn picks or wooden skewers instead for the "handles." Crumbled feta or finely shredded Parmesan are great alternatives to the cotija cheese.

~ ~

8	ears fresh corn with husks
½	cup Duke's Mayonnaise
1	cup crumbled cotija cheese
1	teaspoon chili powder
1	teaspoon paprika
¼	cup chopped fresh cilantro
1	lime, cut into wedges

1. Preheat the grill to medium heat.

2. Pull back the husks on the corn (do not detach) and remove the silks. Replace the husks and soak the ears in cold water for 10 minutes.

3. Remove the corn from the water and shake off the excess. Fold back the husks and tie to create a handle. (Use a torn-off piece of husk as the tie.) Place the ears on the grill and grill for 15 to 20 minutes, turning occasionally, until the corn is tender. Remove from the grill.

4. Brush the corn with the mayonnaise and roll in the cheese. Sprinkle evenly with the chili powder, paprika, and cilantro. Serve with the lime wedges.

Loaded
TWICE-BAKED
Potatoes

MAKES 4 SERVINGS

4	(6-ounce) russet potatoes
1	(8-ounce) block sharp Cheddar cheese, shredded
½	cup Duke's Mayonnaise
8	slices bacon, cooked and crumbled
2	green onions, sliced, plus more for garnish (optional)
¼	teaspoon salt
¼	teaspoon freshly ground pepper

TASTY TIP

Sometimes I'm only able to find ginormous potatoes at the store, so instead of creating Fred Flintstone-size potatoes, I cut the potatoes in half and stuff each half.

For as long as I can remember, my parents have had steak, baked potatoes, and salad or green beans for dinner every Saturday night. When Mom was feeling festive, she would make twice-baked potatoes and they were *the* best. I could make a meal out of them alone. Here's my version, with Duke's of course, crumbled bacon, green onions, and Cheddar.

1. Preheat the oven to 400°F. Prick the potatoes with a fork and place on an aluminum foil–lined rimmed baking sheet. Bake for 45 minutes, or until tender. Let cool slightly.

2. Cut an oval into a flat side of each potato without cutting all the way through. Remove the oval of skin and discard. With a spoon, scoop out the pulp into a bowl, creating four shells.

3. Combine the potato pulp, cheese, mayonnaise, bacon, green onions, salt, and pepper in a medium bowl. Spoon into the potato shells, packing to dome the mixture evenly. Return to the foil-lined baking sheet.

4. Bake the stuffed potatoes at 400°F for 15 to 20 minutes, until the cheese is melted and the potatoes are warmed through. Garnish with additional green onion, if desired.

Fried Brussels Sprouts

with CREAMY HONEY-BALSAMIC DRIZZLE

MAKES 6 TO 8 SERVINGS

If someone you know runs away when Brussels sprouts are mentioned, they haven't tried these. This side is a game changer. My four-year-old gobbled them up like they were potato chips. The edges of the pan-fried sprouts get browned and caramelized, and when paired with the creamy drizzle you'll have a flavor trifecta: salty, sweet, and tangy.

	Creamy Honey-Balsamic Drizzle (recipe follows)
	Peanut oil, for frying
2	pounds Brussels sprouts, trimmed and halved
½	cup all-purpose flour
	Salt

1. Make the Creamy Honey-Balsamic Drizzle.

2. Heat 1 inch of oil in a large cast-iron skillet over medium-high heat to 350°F.

3. Toss the Brussels sprouts with the flour. Fry the Brussels sprouts, in batches, in the hot oil for 2 to 3 minutes, until browned and crispy, shaking the skillet gently to turn the sprouts.

4. Remove the sprouts to paper towels to drain, sprinkling with salt to taste while still hot. Transfer to a serving platter, and drizzle with the Creamy Honey-Balsamic Drizzle.

TASTY TIP

When frying the Brussels sprouts, keep a large lid close by and cover the pan after each batch is added to the hot oil. The moisture from the Brussels sprouts releases naturally and can cause the oil to pop.

Recipe Continues

Creamy
HONEY-BALSAMIC
DRIZZLE

Makes about ²/₃ cup

½ CUP DUKE'S MAYONNAISE

1 TABLESPOON HONEY

1 TABLESPOON WHITE BALSAMIC VINEGAR

¼ TEASPOON SMOKED PAPRIKA

¼ TEASPOON SALT

¼ TEASPOON FRESHLY GROUND PEPPER

Whisk together all the ingredients in a small bowl. Refrigerate
until ready to serve or up to 3 days.

Sweet Potato
au Gratin

MAKES 6 TO 8 SERVINGS

I'm a sucker for potato anything: French fries, baked potatoes, and this sweet potato au gratin. It sounds fancy, but it's actually quite easy to put together and is the perfect side dish for a holiday table. You can try it with Yukon Gold potatoes too.

2	pounds sweet potatoes (about 2 large), peeled and cut into 1/8-inch-thick slices
1½	cups heavy cream
¼	cup Duke's Mayonnaise
½	cup freshly grated Parmesan cheese, divided
1	teaspoon fresh thyme leaves, plus more for garnish (optional)
½	teaspoon salt
½	teaspoon freshly ground pepper
¼	teaspoon ground nutmeg

1. Preheat the oven to 375°F. Lightly grease a 2-quart baking dish.

2. Arrange half of the sweet potatoes in an even layer in the prepared baking dish. Whisk together the cream, mayonnaise, ¼ cup of the cheese, the thyme, salt, pepper, and nutmeg. Pour half of the cream mixture over the sweet potatoes.

3. Top with the remaining sweet potatoes, arranging in an even layer. Pour the remaining cream mixture over the top. Sprinkle with the remaining ¼ cup cheese.

4. Bake the sweet potatoes at 375°F for 40 to 45 minutes, until the sweet potatoes are tender and the mixture is browned and bubbly. Remove from the oven and let stand for 5 minutes before serving. Sprinkle with additional thyme, if desired.

Corn and Basil
Hush Puppies

MAKES 2 DOZEN HUSH PUPPIES

~ ~

My all-time favorite hush puppies (or corn dodgers if you asked my Mimi) were served at what I think was the best seafood dive in all of Savannah: Williams Seafood. Sadly, the restaurant burned down about a decade and a half ago, but I loved going there. When family came to town, that's where we would go to enjoy the best fried shrimp, tartar sauce of course, and hush puppies. I didn't dare try to attempt to re-create them, so instead I've elevated a traditional hush puppy recipe a little with the addition of fresh corn and basil.

~ ~

	Creamy Lemon Dipping Sauce (recipe follows)
	Vegetable oil, for frying
2	cups self-rising yellow cornmeal mix
¼	cup self-rising flour
1	tablespoon sugar

1	cup whole milk
2	tablespoons Duke's Mayonnaise
1	large egg
½	cup fresh corn kernels
⅓	cup chopped fresh basil
	Salt

Recipe Continues

1. Make the Creamy Lemon Dipping Sauce.

2. Pour oil to a depth of 3 inches in a Dutch oven or other large heavy pot. Heat to 375°F over medium-high heat. Place a large rimmed baking sheet layered with paper towels beside the Dutch oven.

3. Stir together the cornmeal mix, flour, and sugar in a medium bowl. Whisk together the milk, mayonnaise, and egg in a separate bowl. Add the milk mixture to the cornmeal mixture, stirring until combined. Fold in the corn and basil.

4. Using a small cookie scoop, spoon the batter into the hot oil in batches and fry for 2 minutes on each side, or until the hush puppies are browned and the insides are done. Remove the hush puppies to the paper towels and sprinkle with salt to taste while still warm. Serve with the Creamy Lemon Dipping Sauce.

TASTY TIP

For easy-to-shuck corn without all those annoying silks,

zap the corn cob—in the husk—in the microwave for about 3 to 4 minutes. Cut off the base of the husk, hold the top of the corn and shake out the cob.

CREAMY LEMON
Dipping Sauce

Makes about ²/₃ cup

¹/₂ **CUP DUKE'S MAYONNAISE**

1 TABLESPOON SOUR CREAM

1 TABLESPOON MINCED SHALLOT

1 TEASPOON GRATED LEMON ZEST

1 TABLESPOON FRESH LEMON JUICE

¹/₄ **TEASPOON PAPRIKA**

Stir together all the ingredients in a small bowl. Refrigerate until ready to serve or up to 3 days.

Tostones

with CILANTRO-JALAPEÑO GREEN SAUCE

MAKES 4 SERVINGS

Also known as _patacones,_ these crispy and starchy snacks hail from Latin America. They were a favorite dish of ours one recent summer when we were in Bocas del Toro, Panama, for my husband's marine science research. If you've never had one before, imagine a giant plantain French fry. They are twice-fried for ultimate crispiness and served with a zesty cilantro sauce that also happens to be awesome on just about anything—from fish tacos to grilled chicken.

	Cilantro-Jalapeño Green Sauce (recipe follows)
	Vegetable oil, for frying
3	**green plantains, peeled and cut into 1-inch-thick pieces**
	Salt

TASTY TIP

Try to pick the greenest unripe plantains you can.

They will be hard to peel, but they make the best tostones. To peel, I use a sharp knife and make a slit down the length of the plantain, then peel away the skin.

1. Make the Cilantro-Jalapeño Green Sauce. Line a rimmed baking sheet with paper towels.

2. Pour oil to a depth of 1 inch in a Dutch oven or other heavy pan and heat over medium-high heat until hot but not smoking. (Test the temperature by dipping a plantain piece in the oil. If it begins to sizzle gently, it's ready.)

3. Fry the plantains in two batches for 3 minutes on each side or until golden. Remove to the paper towel–lined baking sheet.

4. Place each fried plantain between two pieces of parchment paper. Place a cloth on top and flatten the plantain with the heel of your hand to about a ¼-inch thickness (or as flat as you can press it).

5. Return the plantains to the hot oil and fry in two batches for 1 to 2 minutes on each side, until golden brown and crispy. Drain on paper towels, and sprinkle with salt to taste while still hot. Serve with the Cilantro-Jalapeño Green Sauce.

Recipe Continues

CILANTRO-JALAPEÑO
Green Sauce

Makes about 1 cup

³/₄ CUP DUKE'S MAYONNAISE

2 TABLESPOONS FRESH LIME JUICE

1 CUP FRESH CILANTRO LEAVES

2 CLOVES GARLIC, PEELED

1 JALAPEÑO, HALVED AND SEEDED

Process all the ingredients in a food processor or blender until smooth. Refrigerate until ready to serve or up to 3 days.

Rosemary French Fries

with AÏOLI

MAKES 4 TO 6 SERVINGS

The best French fries I ever ate were in a little town near Lucca, Italy. The little house we rented was around the bend of a single-lane road where you'd have to honk the horn to warn oncoming traffic. We heard about a restaurant up the hill, a mom-and-pop joint, that also happened to have a Michelin star, so of course we had to go. As we sat outside at the long wooden table underneath grapevines, waiters brought out platters full of rosemary-scented fries. I'm sure the rest of the meal was delicious, but all I remember was the fries. Here is my attempt to re-create them.

4	russet potatoes, peeled and cut into ¼-inch-thick sticks
	Aïoli (recipe follows)
	Vegetable oil, for frying
8	large sprigs fresh rosemary
	Salt and freshly ground pepper

TASTY TIP

The temperature of the cooking oil is crucial in this recipe. After each batch, make sure the oil returns to the proper heat before frying.

1. Place the potatoes in ice water to cover and refrigerate for at least 2 hours. Drain and pat dry with paper towels. Make the Aïoli while the potatoes chill.

2. Heat the oil in a large Dutch oven or heavy saucepan over medium-high heat to 325°F. Add the rosemary sprigs. Cook the French fries, in batches, for 5 minutes or until lightly golden. Drain on paper towels.

3. Remove the rosemary from the oil and reserve. Increase the oil temperature to 375°F.

4. Cook the French fries, in batches, for 2 to 3 minutes or until golden brown and crisp. Remove to paper towels to drain. Sprinkle with salt and pepper while still hot. Sprinkle the fried rosemary leaves over the top. Serve with the Aïoli for dipping.

Aïoli

Makes about ½ cup

½ CUP DUKE'S MAYONNAISE

¾ TEASPOON FRESH LEMON JUICE

½ TEASPOON DIJON MUSTARD

1 CLOVE GARLIC, MINCED

Stir together all the ingredients in a small bowl.
Refrigerate until ready to serve or up to 3 days.

CHAPTER FIVE

DESSERTS

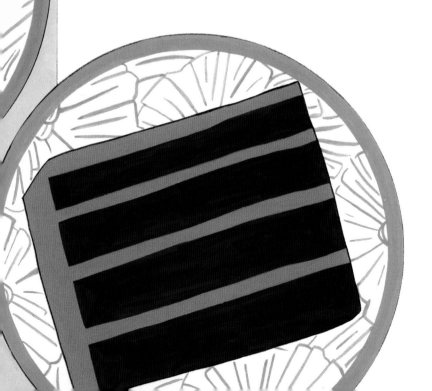

HONG KONG-STYLE
Egg Custard Tarts 208

Thumbprint Cookies 182

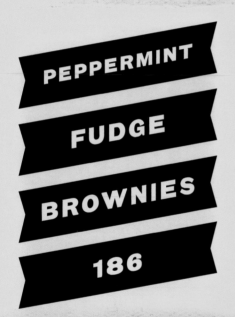

PEPPERMINT

FUDGE

BROWNIES

186

BLACKBERRY AND PEACH CRISP 177

CHEWY CHOCOLATE CHIP COOKIES 176

ICE CREAM COOKIE SANDWICHES 181

MAPLE CUPCAKES
with Candied Bacon 214

Mini Key Lime Pound Cakes 202

Coconut Cream Meringue Tart with Macadamia Nut Crust 225

STICKY TOFFEE PUDDINGS 199

STRAWBERRY-RHUBARB LAYER CAKE 194

TRIPLE CHOCOLATE MOUSSE CAKE 221

MOM'S APPLE PIE 218

Plum Upside-Down Cake 207

GINGERBREAD **BUNDT CAKE** WITH CANDIED GINGER AND ORANGE GLAZE 191

SHOWN ON PAGE 185

Chewy
Chocolate Chip
COOKIES

MAKES 2 DOZEN COOKIES

These chocolate chip cookies are now my go-to recipe. In fact, my mother-in-law claims they are "the best chocolate chip cookies" she's ever had. I'll take it! They are the perfect combination of chewy centers with slightly crunchy bottoms, making them ideal for ice cream sandwiches. I like to use a cookie scoop for ease of cleanup and uniform baking.

2	**cups all-purpose flour**
2	**teaspoons cornstarch**
½	**teaspoon baking soda**
	Pinch of salt
¾	**cup Duke's Mayonnaise**
½	**cup firmly packed light brown sugar**
½	**cup granulated sugar**
1	**large egg**
2	**teaspoons vanilla extract**
1	**cup bittersweet chocolate chunks or chips**

1. Preheat the oven to 350°F. Line two rimmed baking sheets with parchment paper.

2. Stir together the flour, cornstarch, baking soda, and salt in a small bowl.

3. Whisk together the mayonnaise, sugars, egg, and vanilla in a medium bowl until the mixture is smooth. Add the flour mixture and stir until combined. Fold in the chocolate chunks.

4. Using a small cookie scoop, scoop the dough into 24 balls. Or, roll the dough into 24 (1½-inch) balls. Place the dough balls 2 inches apart on the prepared baking sheets.

5. Bake the cookies at 350°F for 12 to 14 minutes, until the bottoms and edges of the cookies are lightly golden. Let cool on the baking sheets for 5 minutes before removing to wire racks to cool.

BLACKBERRY *and* Peach Crisp

MAKES 6 TO 8 SERVINGS

There were several consecutive summers, starting when I was about 10, when my family and my aunt, uncle, and cousins stayed in a cabin on Lake Glenville, North Carolina. The cousins would stay up late at night, peeking down from the loft onto the dining table where our parents played Spades. At first light in the mornings, we would race out the door to see who could find the most wild blackberries. By the end of the week, we would have gathered enough to make a small crisp or cobbler, and it was always the best. Here, I've added a natural partner to blackberries: peaches. This is equally delicious by itself or with scoops of vanilla ice cream on top.

	Brown Sugar–Oatmeal Topping (recipe follows)
3	cups fresh blackberries
3	large peaches, peeled and sliced
1	tablespoon fresh lemon juice
2	tablespoons granulated sugar
2	tablespoons cornstarch
	Vanilla ice cream (optional)

1. Preheat the oven to 350°F. Make the Brown Sugar–Oatmeal Topping.

2. Toss together the blackberries, peaches, lemon juice, sugar, and cornstarch in a large bowl. Transfer to a large ovenproof skillet or 2-quart baking dish. Top evenly with the Brown Sugar–Oatmeal Topping.

3. Bake the crisp at 350°F for 35 to 40 minutes, until the topping is browned and the fruit mixture is bubbly. Remove from the oven and serve warm with ice cream, if desired.

TASTY TIP

So many fruits would work in place of the peaches and blackberries here if they're in season. You can also use thawed frozen fruit if you'd like.

Recipe Continues

BROWN SUGAR-OATMEAL
Topping

Makes about 3 cups

1 CUP ALL-PURPOSE FLOUR

1 CUP OLD-FASHIONED OATS

1 CUP FIRMLY PACKED BROWN SUGAR

1 TEASPOON GROUND CINNAMON

$^3/_4$ CUP DUKE'S MAYONNAISE

Stir together all the ingredients in a medium bowl.
Squeeze the mixture to create large clumps.

Ice Cream
Cookie
SANDWICHES

MAKES 15 ICE CREAM SANDWICHES

2¾	cups all-purpose flour
1	teaspoon baking soda
½	teaspoon baking powder
½	teaspoon cornstarch
1½	cups granulated sugar
1	cup Duke's Mayonnaise
1	large egg
2	teaspoons vanilla extract
	Coarse sugar (optional)
	Favorite ice creams
	Sprinkles (optional)

TASTY TIP

How food stylists make even ice cream centers:

Soften the ice cream and spread onto a rimmed baking sheet. Freeze for 1 to 2 hours, or until firm. Use a round biscuit cutter the same size as the cookies to cut out even ice cream rounds.

Let me tell you, I am typically not a sugar cookie fan. But boy do I love the sugar cookies in this recipe. Have you ever sunk your teeth into an ice cream sandwich and the ice cream squishes out the sides because the cookies are too hard? It's the worst! These cookies are soft and chewy with a crunchy sugar topping and are made to sandwich ice cream (without the squishing). I love to fill these with fruity concoctions like frozen lemon custard or sherbet, but use your favorite frozen treat.

1. Preheat the oven to 350°F. Line two rimmed baking sheets with parchment paper.

2. Stir together the flour, baking soda, baking powder, and cornstarch in a medium bowl.

3. Beat the granulated sugar and mayonnaise with an electric mixer until creamy; add the egg and beat until the yellow disappears. Beat in the vanilla.

4. Add the flour mixture to the mayonnaise mixture and beat until combined. Using a small cookie scoop, scoop the dough into 30 balls. Or roll the dough into 30 (1½-inch) balls. Roll in the coarse sugar, if desired, and place on the baking sheets 2 inches apart.

5. Bake the cookies at 350°F for 14 to 16 minutes, until the bottoms are lightly golden. (Don't overbake or the cookies will become hard.) Let cool on the baking sheets on a wire rack.

6. Sandwich about ⅓ cup ice cream between two cookies. Roll the edges in sprinkles, if desired. Wrap the sandwiches individually and freeze, or serve immediately.

Thumbprint
Cookies

MAKES 2 DOZEN COOKIES

If you're a cookie baker, you should add this recipe to your repertoire. Shortbread filled with jewel-toned jam makes for a pretty presentation, whether for cookie swaps during the holidays or to just enjoy with a cup of tea. They're also great to make with the little ones in your life. Small hands are just the right size for making the indentions for the jam.

½	cup unsalted butter, softened
⅔	cup granulated sugar, plus more for rolling
¼	cup Duke's Mayonnaise
1	large egg
2⅓	cups all-purpose flour
¼	teaspoon salt
1	teaspoon vanilla extract
½	cup favorite jam or lemon curd

1. Preheat the oven to 375°F. Line a rimmed baking sheet with parchment paper.

2. Beat the butter, sugar, and mayonnaise with an electric mixer until creamy. Add the egg and beat just until the yellow disappears.

3. Stir together the flour and salt. Add to the butter mixture and beat just until combined. Beat in the vanilla.

4. Roll the dough into 24 (1-inch) balls. Roll each dough ball in additional sugar and place on the prepared baking sheet.

5. Use your thumb or the handle of a wooden spoon to make a small indention in the center of each dough ball.

6. Microwave the jam or lemon curd for 15 to 30 seconds, just until melted. Spoon about 1 teaspoon jam into the indention in each cookie.

7. Bake the cookies at 375°F for 10 to 12 minutes, until the cookies are set and the bottoms are lightly golden. Remove to wire racks to cool.

The first thing I fell in love with when I moved to Georgia was Duke's Mayonnaise. Somehow I had missed meeting it before and, returning from England, it was a total surprise with my first locally grown Georgia tomato sandwich. There was a lovely unexpected zip to the sandwich, I swooned, and that was the beginning of my devotion. As Ashley shows in this delightful book, there is nothing like Duke's.

—NATHALIE DUPREE, JAMES BEARD AWARD–WINNING COOKBOOK AUTHOR

Thumbprint
Cookies,
PAGE 182

Peppermint
Fudge
Brownies,
PAGE 186

Chewy
Chocolate
Chip Cookies,
PAGE 176

SHOWN ON PAGE 185

Peppermint Fudge Brownies

MAKES 16 BROWNIES

~ ~

You know that famous chocolate and peppermint bark sold around the holidays? It's the inspiration behind these fudgy brownies. The brownies are actually quite delicious on their own, but topping them with a creamy peppermint frosting, pools of dark chocolate, and crushed peppermints takes them to a whole new level. If you're in a hurry, you can pop the just-topped brownies in the fridge for 15 minutes to allow the chocolate to harden before cutting.

~ ~

¾	cup all-purpose flour		2	large eggs
¼	cup cocoa powder		1	teaspoon vanilla extract
1	teaspoon baking powder		1	cup semisweet chocolate chips, melted
½	teaspoon salt			Peppermint Frosting (recipe follows)
1	cup granulated sugar			Chocolate Drizzle (recipe follows)
½	cup Duke's Mayonnaise			Crushed peppermints

1. Preheat the oven to 325°F. Line an 8-inch baking pan with parchment paper, extending the paper 2 inches over the sides to act as handles for easy lifting after the brownies have baked.

2. Stir together the flour, cocoa powder, baking powder, and salt in a medium bowl. Stir together the sugar, mayonnaise, eggs, and vanilla in a large bowl. Add the flour mixture to the sugar mixture, stirring until combined. Stir in the melted chocolate.

3. Bake the brownies at 325°F for 40 minutes, or until a toothpick inserted 1 inch from an edge comes out clean. Remove to a wire rack to cool completely. While the brownies cool, make the Peppermint Frosting and the Chocolate Drizzle.

4. Use the parchment handles to lift the brownies from the pan. Remove the parchment paper. Spread the Peppermint Frosting evenly over the brownies. Spoon the Chocolate Drizzle over the frosting, and sprinkle with crushed peppermints. Let stand until the chocolate hardens (or refrigerate for 15 minutes). Cut into 16 squares.

Recipe Continues

Peppermint FROSTING

Makes about ²/₃ cup

¼ CUP SALTED BUTTER, SOFTENED

1 CUP POWDERED SUGAR

1 TO 2 TEASPOONS WHOLE MILK

¼ TEASPOON PEPPERMINT EXTRACT

Beat the butter at medium speed with an electric
mixer until creamy. Add the powdered sugar and beat
until fluffy. Add 1 teaspoon milk and beat until the
mixture is smooth; add more milk if needed. Beat in
the peppermint extract.

Chocolate DRIZZLE

Makes about ½ cup

¼ CUP UNSALTED BUTTER

½ CUP SEMISWEET CHOCOLATE CHIPS

Place the butter and chocolate chips in a
microwave-safe dish. Microwave at HIGH in 30-second
intervals until the butter and chocolate are melted.
Stir until smooth. Let cool until the chocolate
is drizzling consistency.

Gingerbread Bundt Cake

with CANDIED GINGER AND ORANGE GLAZE

MAKES 10 TO 12 SERVINGS

2	(14.5-ounce) packages gingerbread cake and cookie mix
1½	cups Duke's Mayonnaise
1	teaspoon ground ginger
1	teaspoon ground cinnamon
1½	cups water
3	large eggs
1	teaspoon vanilla extract
	Orange Glaze (recipe follows)
	Candied crystalized ginger and orange zest curls

I am not a baker. There, I said it. There's too much measuring or calculating if something doesn't work. A baking recipe has to be either super-easy or so delicious that the work is worth it. That's why this recipe is so great. It's a cake mix that's been doctored up with impressive decorations. So serve this at your next holiday gathering and impress everyone. Secret's safe with me.

1. Preheat the oven to 350°F. Grease and flour a Bundt pan (I use vegetable shortening).

2. Beat the gingerbread mixes, mayonnaise, ginger, and cinnamon with an electric mixer until combined. Add the water, eggs, and vanilla and beat until the batter is smooth. Pour into the prepared Bundt pan.

3. Bake the cake at 350°F for 50 to 53 minutes, until a toothpick inserted in the center comes out clean. Let cool in the pan for 5 minutes. Run a knife around the edge and center and turn the cake out onto a wire rack to cool completely.

4. While the cake cools, make the Orange Glaze. Drizzle the cake with the Orange Glaze, and sprinkle with crystalized ginger and orange zest curls.

Recipe Continues

Orange GLAZE

Makes ½ cup

1½ CUPS POWDERED SUGAR

1 TO 2 TABLESPOONS FRESH
ORANGE JUICE

½ TEASPOON VANILLA EXTRACT

Stir together the powdered sugar, 1 tablespoon orange
juice, and vanilla in a small bowl until smooth. Add
additional orange juice, if desired, for a thinner glaze.

I would rather take a whole dish off the menu than substitute something else for Duke's Mayo. That is the level of difference I believe it makes in every dish we put it in.

—KATIE COSS, EXECUTIVE CHEF AT HUSK IN NASHVILLE, TENNESSEE

STRAWBERRY-RHUBARB
Layer Cake

MAKES 8 TO 10 SERVINGS

2	(16.25-ounce) boxes white cake mix
2	cups Duke's Mayonnaise
6	large eggs
2	cups water
1	teaspoon vanilla extract
½	teaspoon almond extract
	Strawberry-Rhubarb Filling (recipe follows)
	Strawberry-Rhubarb Buttercream (recipe follows)
	Fresh strawberries (optional)

What I love about this cake is that it all starts with cake mix and transforms into a delicious and impressive layer cake. I like to make the cake layers first, and while they are baking I focus on the filling. (Don't forget to set aside ½ cup filling to use in the buttercream.) My oven isn't large enough to fit three cake pans on one rack, so I bake two cakes first and the third by itself after the first two are out of the oven.

1. Preheat the oven to 350°F. Grease (I use vegetable shortening) and flour 3 (9-inch) cake pans.

2. Beat together the cake mixes, mayonnaise, and eggs in a large bowl with an electric mixer until combined. Beat in the water and extracts. Beat for 2 minutes, or until the batter is smooth.

3. Divide the batter evenly among the prepared cake pans. Bake the cakes at 350°F for 26 to 28 minutes, until a toothpick inserted in the center comes out clean. Let cool in the pans for 5 minutes. Run a knife around the edges of the cakes and turn them out onto wire racks to cool completely.

4. While the cakes are baking and cooling, make the Strawberry-Rhubarb Filling. Set aside ½ cup filling for the Strawberry-Rhubarb Buttercream. Make the Strawberry-Rhubarb Buttercream.

5. Place one cake on a cake plate or stand. Spread about 1¼ cups Strawberry-Rhubarb Filling over the top and almost to the edges. (Don't spread all the way; any filling around the edges of the cake will make it hard to spread the buttercream frosting.) Place another cake on top and repeat the process. Place the remaining cake on top.

6. Spread the Strawberry-Rhubarb Buttercream on the top and sides of the cake. Decorate with fresh strawberries, if desired.

Recipe Continues

STRAWBERRY-RHUBARB *Filling*

Makes about 3 cups

1 POUND FRESH RHUBARB, CHOPPED

1 POUND FRESH STRAWBERRIES, HULLED AND HALVED

1 CUP GRANULATED SUGAR

2 TABLESPOONS WATER

Combine all the ingredients in a heavy medium saucepan over medium-high heat. Simmer for 15 to 20 minutes, until the mixture thickens to jam consistency. (To test, dip a wooden spoon in the mixture and let cool slightly. Run your finger through the center of the jam: If the line remains without any bleeding, the filling is done.) Let cool.

TASTY TIP

Rhubarb is a spring and summertime crop, so if you can't find fresh, frozen is a great substitute. Just be sure to thaw it first.

STRAWBERRY-RHUBARB
Buttercream

Makes about 3 cups

1 CUP SALTED BUTTER, SOFTENED

4 TO 4¹⁄₂ CUPS POWDERED SUGAR

¹⁄₂ CUP STRAWBERRY-RHUBARB FILLING

¹⁄₂ TEASPOON VANILLA EXTRACT

1. Beat the butter in a large bowl at medium speed with an electric mixer until creamy. Add 4 cups powdered sugar and beat until combined.

2. Add the filling and vanilla extract; beat until the mixture is fluffy. Add an additional ½ cup powdered sugar, if necessary, to reach a spreading consistency.

Sticky
TOFFEE
Puddings
MAKES 8 SERVINGS

~ ~

A few summers ago, our family went to Ireland and I had the best sticky toffee pudding I'd ever had. Granted, it was probably the second or third time I'd ever had the dessert, but it was one food memory of our trip that stands out. We had been driving all day to Dingle and, even though it was June, it was cold and rainy out. We were meeting the homeowner of the house we were renting at Murphy's Pub, and after getting the keys to the house, we decided to sit down for an Irish coffee and something to eat. As soon as I saw sticky toffee pudding on the menu, I knew we had to order it. Perfectly spongy and just-from-the-oven warm, the small cake was drenched in a silky caramel sauce and was made even better by a scoop of vanilla ice cream. I had to try and re-create the dessert at home. It's actually quite an easy cake to make but nonetheless very impressive.

~ ~

½	cup pitted dates (about 5)		½	cup granulated sugar
¾	cup boiling water		2	tablespoons packed dark brown sugar
¾	teaspoon baking soda		¼	teaspoon salt
	Toffee Sauce (recipe follows)		1	cup all-purpose flour
½	cup Duke's Mayonnaise		1¼	teaspoons baking powder

Recipe Continues

1. Preheat the oven to 350°F. Grease 8 (4-ounce) popover cups, ramekins, or custard molds.

2. Combine the dates, boiling water, and baking soda in a medium bowl. Let stand for 30 minutes. Process in a blender until smooth. Make the Toffee Sauce while the mixture stands.

3. Beat the mayonnaise, sugars, and salt in a mixer until fluffy. Stir together the flour and baking powder. Add the flour mixture to the mayonnaise mixture alternately with the date mixture, beginning and ending with the flour mixture.

4. Pour the batter into the prepared cups or molds. Bake the puddings at 350°F for 20 to 25 minutes, until a toothpick inserted in the center comes out clean. Let cool on a wire rack for 5 minutes; unmold and top each serving with Toffee Sauce.

Toffee SAUCE

Makes about 2 cups

½ CUP SALTED BUTTER

1 CUP HEAVY CREAM

1 CUP FIRMLY PACKED DARK BROWN SUGAR

2 TEASPOONS VANILLA EXTRACT

Melt the butter in a medium saucepan over medium heat; add the cream and brown sugar. Bring to a boil; reduce the heat and simmer for 15 to 20 minutes, until the sauce begins to thicken. Stir in the vanilla.

As a mother, I want my children to learn what's important in life. That's why we eat Duke's Mayonnaise in our house.

—VIVIAN HOWARD, JAMES BEARD AWARD–WINNING AUTHOR, CHEF, AND TV PERSONALITY

Mini
KEY LIME
Pound Cakes

**MAKES 10 BUNDTLETTES
(OR 16 MUFFIN-SIZE CAKES)**

~~~~~~~~~~~~~~~~~~~~~~

When we lived in South Florida, we had the opportunity to visit the Florida Keys a handful of times. If you've ever driven along Highway 1 from Miami, you know it's a lot longer of a drive than one might think. The first key you come to, Key Largo, is home to Mrs. Mac's Kitchen, a restaurant that I think serves *the* best key lime pie. We always stopped there for a bite before heading on to Marathon or another key, and likely stopped again on the way home to pick up a whole pie. This recipe combines the flavors of key lime pie with another one of my favorite desserts: pound cake. I tested the recipe with Nordic Ware's Bundtlette pans because of how cute the mini cakes are, but I also include instructions for baking in a muffin pan.

~~~~~~~~~~~~~~~~~~~~~~

2	cups all-purpose flour	1	teaspoon vanilla extract
2	teaspoons baking powder	1	teaspoon grated key lime zest (or regular lime zest)
¼	teaspoon salt	½	cup whole milk
1¾	cups granulated sugar		Key Lime Glaze (recipe follows)
¼	cup Duke's Mayonnaise		Key lime slices (optional)
4	large eggs		

Recipe Continues

1. Preheat the oven to 350°F. Grease (I use vegetable shortening) and flour 10 mini Bundt pan cups (Bundtlettes) or 16 muffin cups.

2. Combine the flour, baking powder, and salt in a small bowl. Beat the sugar and mayonnaise with an electric mixer at medium speed until creamy. Add the eggs, one at a time, beating well after each addition. Beat in the vanilla and lime zest.

3. Add the flour mixture to the sugar mixture alternately with the milk, beginning and ending with the flour mixture. Divide the batter evenly among the Bundt pan cups or muffin cups, filling each three-quarters full.

4. Bake the cakes at 350°F for 20 to 23 minutes, until a toothpick inserted in the center comes out clean. Remove the pan from the oven. Run a knife around the edges of the cakes and immediately remove the cakes to a wire rack to cool completely.

5. While the cakes cool, make the Key Lime Glaze.

6. Drizzle the cakes with the Key Lime Glaze before serving. Garnish with lime slices, if desired.

Key Lime GLAZE

Makes about ²/₃ cup

¾ CUP POWDERED SUGAR

1 TEASPOON GRATED KEY LIME ZEST (OR REGULAR LIME ZEST)

1 TO 2 TABLESPOONS KEY LIME JUICE (OR REGULAR LIME JUICE)

Stir together all the ingredients in a small bowl until smooth.

TASTY TIP

If you can't find key limes, use Persian limes instead.

Duke's Mayonnaise is the quintessential Southern condiment because it's the perfect balance of sweet, tangy, and creamy.

—CARLA HALL, CHEF, AUTHOR, AND TELEVISION PERSONALITY

Plum
UPSIDE-DOWN
Cake

MAKES 8 TO 10 SERVINGS

¼	cup salted butter
½	cup firmly packed light brown sugar
¼	teaspoon ground cinnamon
3	black or red plums, pitted and thinly sliced
2	cups all-purpose flour
1	teaspoon baking powder
¼	teaspoon salt
1	cup granulated sugar
1	cup Duke's Mayonnaise
3	large eggs
½	cup whole milk
1	teaspoon vanilla extract
½	teaspoon almond extract

Move over pineapple upside-down cake—a new version is in town. This secretly easy, impressive dessert is all about the layering of the fruit. Note that super-ripe plums actually work better, and arranging them in a single layer is key. You'll also want to turn the cake out (upside-down) while it's still hot, and let it cool on the serving plate.

1. Preheat the oven to 350°F. Grease a 9-inch round baking pan (I use vegetable shortening).

2. Combine the butter, brown sugar, and cinnamon in a small saucepan. Place over medium heat and cook until the butter is melted, stirring until smooth. Pour the mixture into the prepared cake pan, spreading to coat evenly.

3. Arrange the plum slices in a single layer in concentric circles over the brown sugar mixture. (I make one circle in the center and one around the edges.)

4. Stir together the flour, baking powder, and salt in a small bowl. Set aside.

5. Beat the granulated sugar and mayonnaise with an electric mixer until creamy. Add the eggs, one at a time, beating well after each addition. Add the flour mixture to the sugar mixture alternately with the milk, beginning and ending with the flour mixture. Beat in the extracts.

6. Pour the batter evenly over the plums. Bake the cake at 350°F for 40 to 45 minutes, until a toothpick inserted in the center comes out clean. Let cool in the pan for 5 minutes.

7. Run a knife around the edge and immediately turn out the cake onto a rimmed cake plate or platter. Serve warm or at room temperature.

Egg Custard Tarts

MAKES 22 TARTS

You may have tried or seen the cousin to these little two-bite tarts, Portuguese tarts. I hadn't had one until we lived in Hong Kong. One day during the beginning of our time there, we were walking around exploring the Central District, and I caught a whiff of the pastries. As we passed by the little shop, I knew I had to try one. A flaky, slightly sweet shortcrust pastry enveloped a creamy, still-warm custard filling. I was hooked. Over the next several months I would find myself in that same neighborhood and had to— of course—buy one. I often suffered from "burned-roof-of-mouth syndrome" because I couldn't wait for the tarts to cool before digging in.

	Sweet Pastry Dough (recipe follows)		2	large eggs
⅔	cup water		⅓	cup evaporated milk
⅓	cup granulated sugar		1	teaspoon vanilla extract

Recipe Continues

1. Make the Sweet Pastry Dough.

2. Preheat the oven to 350°F. Grease 22 mini (2-inch diameter) fluted egg tart molds or 22 wells in muffin tins. (I use vegetable shortening.)

3. Roll out the Sweet Pastry Dough to ⅛-inch thickness. Using a 2½-inch round cutter, cut the dough into 22 rounds, rerolling as needed. Press the dough rounds into each tart mold or muffin cup.

4. Bring the water and sugar to a boil in a small saucepan and heat until the sugar dissolves.

5. Whisk together the eggs, milk, and vanilla in a medium bowl. While whisking, slowly pour the sugar water into the egg mixture.

6. Pour the filling through a strainer into a measuring cup with a pouring spout. Pour the strained custard into the pastry shells. Bake the pastries on the bottom rack at 350°F for 18 to 20 minutes (if using egg tart molds) or 15 to 17 minutes (if using muffin tins). The pastries are done when the filling is glossy and set. Remove the pans to wire racks and cool in the pans. Run a knife tip around the edges and unmold.

TASTY TIP

Be careful not to allow any of the egg filling to spill over the sides of the pastry. It'll make unmolding them more difficult because they may stick.

Sweet
PASTRY DOUGH

Makes enough dough for 22 small tarts

2 CUPS ALL-PURPOSE FLOUR

¼ CUP POWDERED SUGAR

½ CUP DUKE'S MAYONNAISE

3 TABLESPOONS COLD WATER

1. Pulse the flour, sugar, and mayonnaise in a food processor until the mixture is sandy. With the motor running, add the water through the food chute, 1 tablespoon at a time, until the mixture forms a dough.

2. Shape the dough into a disk and let rest at room temperature for 30 minutes. (Or refrigerate until ready to use. Let stand at room temperature for 1 hour or until pliable.)

Put Up Your Duke's. It's not news
that most Southern cooks and eaters
are fiercely loyal to our Duke's. It's a
matter of taste and decorum. Duke's is
the brand that many of us Southerners
grew up on, so it's the mayo that
tastes like what we expect and crave.
Most food memories of this caliber
require the replication of a prized
family recipe, but Duke's requires
only the twist of that signature
bright yellow lid. Each new jar is a
fresh start full of promise, a legacy
and luxury for about four bucks a

pop. Duke's Mayonnaise has inspired art, poetry, essays, scholarly treatises, lectures, and quarrels with those who prefer other brands or think it doesn't matter. (I was once married to a man who wouldn't touch mayonnaise but liked Miracle Whip. It's not the reason we parted, but it speaks to motive.) Thank you kindly, Ms. Eugenia, for bestowing Duke's Mayonnaise on us, the spread that binds countless Southern recipes and graces more 'mater sandwiches than there are stars in the heavens.

—SHERI CASTLE, COOKBOOK AUTHOR, FOOD WRITER, RECIPE DEVELOPER, AND STORYTELLER

Maple
Cupcakes
with CANDIED BACON

MAKES 16 CUPCAKES

I have to give all the credit for the idea of these cupcakes to my husband, Chris. One of our favorite doughnut places in Charleston is Duck Donuts, and on their menu is a Maple-Bacon doughnut. The saltiness of the bacon is the perfect complement to sweet maple frosting. When I was thinking of cupcake ideas, Chris's solution was: Bacon! Why not make a bacon cupcake? I was intrigued and immediately thought of his doughnut choice (and often mine). I took it one step further and created candied bacon to adorn the over-the-top cupcakes. Also note that the bacon would be a great addition to any breakfast or brunch spread.

	Candied Bacon (recipe follows)
¼	cup salted butter
2	cups all-purpose flour
1½	teaspoons baking powder
½	teaspoon baking soda
¼	teaspoon salt
¾	cup Duke's Mayonnaise
1	cup firmly packed brown sugar
¼	cup granulated sugar
1	cup whole milk
1	teaspoon vanilla extract
½	teaspoon maple extract
	Maple Frosting (recipe follows)

1. Make the Candied Bacon.

2. Preheat the oven to 350°F. Line 16 wells in muffin tins with paper liners.

3. Cook the butter in a small skillet over medium heat for 2 to 3 minutes, swirling the pan occasionally, until the milk solids begin to brown and smell nutty. Set aside.

4. Combine the flour, baking powder, baking soda, and salt in a medium bowl.

5. Beat the browned butter, mayonnaise, and sugars with an electric mixer until creamy. Add the flour mixture to the browned butter mixture alternately with the milk, beginning and ending with the flour mixture. Stir in the extracts.

6. Divide the batter evenly among the muffin liners. Bake the cupcakes at 350°F for 19 to 22 minutes, until a toothpick inserted in the center comes out clean. Remove to wire racks to cool.

7. While the cupcakes cool, make the Maple Frosting.

8. Pipe or spread the Maple Frosting onto the cupcakes. Top with pieces of Candied Bacon.

Recipe Continues

Candied
BACON

Makes 8 slices

8 SLICES THICK-CUT BACON

$\frac{1}{3}$ CUP FIRMLY PACKED LIGHT BROWN SUGAR

2 TABLESPOONS APPLE CIDER VINEGAR

2 TABLESPOONS MAPLE SYRUP

1. Preheat the oven to 350°F. Line a rimmed baking sheet with parchment paper or a Silpat.

2. Arrange the bacon in a single layer on the lined baking sheet. Bake for 10 minutes; turn and cook for 5 more minutes.

3. Combine the brown sugar, vinegar, and maple syrup in a small bowl.

4. Brush the bacon with one-third of the brown sugar mixture. Bake for 10 minutes.

5. Turn the bacon; brush with another one-third of the mixture. Bake for 10 minutes.

6. Brush with the remaining mixture. Bake for 10 more minutes, until the bacon fat is translucent and the bacon meat is browned. (The bacon will not be crisp.) Remove to parchment paper to cool. (The bacon will harden as it cools.) Cut each slice in half crosswise.

Maple FROSTING

Makes about 2 cups

½ CUP SALTED BUTTER, SOFTENED

½ CUP FIRMLY PACKED LIGHT BROWN SUGAR

⅓ CUP MAPLE SYRUP

3 CUPS POWDERED SUGAR

1 TO 2 TABLESPOONS WHOLE MILK

1 TEASPOON MAPLE EXTRACT

1. Bring the butter, brown sugar, and maple syrup to a boil in a small saucepan over medium-high heat. Boil for 5 minutes, stirring constantly, until the sugar is dissolved. Let cool completely.

2. Beat the cooled butter mixture with the powdered sugar with an electric mixer until combined. Add the milk and maple extract and beat until creamy.

TASTY TIP

Maple extract can sometimes be tricky to find, but it is a crucial ingredient in this recipe. You can order it online, or I've found it at Food Lion, Bi-Lo, and Walmart grocery stores.

SHOWN ON PAGE 115

Mom's
Apple Pie

MAKES 8 TO 10 SERVINGS

My mom is known for her apple pie. It's one of those recipes that if she doesn't make it at Christmas or Thanksgiving, someone will pout and complain, and she'll never hear the end of it. To prevent a soggy crust, her secret is to first cook the apples on the stovetop to thicken the juice. Paired with my flaky sweet pie crust (Duke's is the secret ingredient), everyone will want this pie to grace their holiday or Sunday supper table. To save time, make the pie dough first and then cook your apple filling while it rests.

	Double-Crust Sweet Pastry Dough (recipe follows)
7	Pink Lady, Honeycrisp, or sweet red apples (each about 7 ounces; total around 3 pounds), cored, peeled, and sliced (about 8 cups)
½	cup firmly packed light brown sugar
½	cup granulated sugar
2	teaspoons ground cinnamon
½	teaspoon ground nutmeg
2	tablespoons cornstarch
1	tablespoon fresh lemon juice
1	tablespoon vanilla extract
2	tablespoons salted butter, cut up
1	large egg
1	teaspoon water

1. Make the Double-Crust Sweet Pastry Dough.

2. Combine the sliced apples, sugars, cinnamon, and nutmeg in a large stockpot or Dutch oven. Cook over medium heat for 25 minutes, or until the juices release and the apples begin to soften, stirring occasionally.

3. Preheat the oven to 450°F. Stir together the cornstarch, lemon juice, and vanilla. Add to the apples and cook for about 5 minutes, or until the sauce is thickened.

4. Roll out one dough portion to a 10-inch round and fit into a 9-inch pie plate. Top with the apples and dot with the butter.

5. Roll out the remaining dough portion into a 10-inch round. Cut into strips, if desired, to create a lattice. Or, cut a hole in the center to act as an air vent. Arrange the lattice or dough round on top of the apples. Fold the edges under and crimp to seal.

6. Whisk together the egg and water; brush all over the pie dough.

7. Bake the pie at 450°F for 10 minutes. Reduce the oven temperature to 350°F and bake for 35 more minutes, or until the crust is browned. Remove from the oven and serve warm or at room temperature.

DOUBLE-CRUST SWEET PASTRY Dough

Makes enough dough for 2 (9-inch) pie crusts

4 CUPS ALL-PURPOSE FLOUR

½ CUP POWDERED SUGAR

1 CUP DUKE'S MAYONNAISE

6 TABLESPOONS COLD WATER

1. Pulse the flour and sugar in a food processor until combined. Add the mayonnaise and pulse until the mixture is sandy.

2. With the motor running, slowly add the water, 1 tablespoon at a time, through the food chute and process just until a dough forms.

3. Divide the dough into two balls and shape each into a disk. Wrap and let rest at room temperature for 30 minutes. (Or refrigerate until ready to use. Let stand at room temperature for 1 hour or until pliable.)

Triple Chocolate Mousse CAKE

MAKES 8 TO 10 SERVINGS

~ ~

Okay, this is the ultimate cake for chocoholics, and I happen to be one. You know how I mentioned that I don't like to bake unless the recipe is worth it? This recipe is worth it, in spades. You may have heard of the famous chocolate mayonnaise cake. This is my version, kicked up several notches. The cake, with its luscious texture and moisture from Duke's, is filled with layers of fluffy chocolate mousse and enveloped in a rich ganache frosting. I'm a dark chocolate lover so I've used bittersweet chocolate, but if you like a sweeter chocolate, opt for semisweet or milk chocolate for just as delicious results.

~ ~

2	cups all-purpose flour	1	cup granulated sugar
½	cup sifted cocoa powder, plus more for dusting	3	large eggs
1¼	teaspoons baking soda	1¼	cups water
¼	teaspoon baking powder	1	teaspoon vanilla extract
	Pinch of salt		Ganache Frosting (recipe follows)
1	cup Duke's Mayonnaise		Chocolate Mousse Filling (recipe follows)

Recipe Continues

1. Preheat the oven to 350°F. Grease two (8-inch) round cake pans (I use vegetable shortening) and dust with cocoa powder.

2. Stir together the flour, cocoa powder, baking soda, baking powder, and salt in a medium bowl.

3. Beat the mayonnaise and sugar with an electric mixer until creamy. Add the eggs, one at a time, until combined. Add the flour mixture alternately with the water, beginning and ending with the flour mixture. Beat at medium-low speed for 1 minute. (Batter will be thin.) Stir in the vanilla.

4. Pour the batter evenly into the prepared pans. Bake the cakes at 350°F for 21 to 24 minutes, until a toothpick inserted in the center comes out clean. Remove to wire racks. Let cool in the pans for 5 minutes. Run a knife around the edges and turn out onto wire racks to cool completely. Once cooled, split each layer in half.

5. Make the Ganache Frosting and the Chocolate Mousse Filling.

6. Place one cake layer on a cake plate or stand. Top with one-third of the Chocolate Mousse Filling; repeat the process twice. Place the remaining cake layer on top. Spread the Ganache Frosting on the top and sides of the cake before slicing.

GANACHE
Frosting

Makes about 2 cups

8 OUNCES BITTERSWEET CHOCOLATE, CHOPPED

³/₄ CUP HEAVY CREAM

1¹/₂ TABLESPOONS CORN SYRUP

1. Place the chocolate in a medium bowl. Heat the cream and corn syrup in a small saucepan until the cream is hot. Pour over the chocolate. Let stand for 1 minute, then stir until smooth.

2. For a shiny look, let stand until spreadable (20 to 30 minutes), stirring occasionally. For fluffy chocolate frosting, beat the mixture with an electric mixer until fluffy.

CHOCOLATE MOUSSE *Filling*

Makes about 3 cups

1¹/₂ TEASPOONS UNFLAVORED GELATIN

1 TABLESPOON COLD WATER

1 TABLESPOON BOILING WATER

6 OUNCES BITTERSWEET CHOCOLATE, CHOPPED

1¹/₂ CUPS HEAVY CREAM, DIVIDED

2 TABLESPOONS GRANULATED SUGAR

1. Sprinkle the gelatin over the cold water in a small bowl. Let stand until the gelatin softens. Stir in the boiling water to dissolve the gelatin.

2. Place the chocolate in a medium bowl. Heat ½ cup of the cream and the sugar in a small saucepan over medium heat until the sugar dissolves and the cream is steaming. Pour over the chopped chocolate; add the gelatin and stir until smooth.

3. Beat the remaining 1 cup cream with an electric mixer until stiff peaks form. Fold a small amount of whipped cream into the chocolate; gently fold in the remaining whipped cream until combined. Use immediately. (The mixture will firm up as it stands.)

Duke's is the secret sauce that turned this life-long mayo hater into a mayo maniac—with one strict proviso: It's Duke's or nothing. My family loves the tangy, creamy, yummy taste trifecta Duke's brings to all our favorite dishes.

—MARY KAY ANDREWS, AUTHOR

Coconut Cream
Meringue Tart

with MACADAMIA NUT CRUST

MAKES 8 TO 10 SERVINGS

Kauai is where my mother-in-law lives, and it's one of our happy places. If you're ever in Hawaii, you should visit the pie lady from The Right Slice on the island of Kauai. I always choose *lilikoi* (passion fruit) or coconut cream pie from the dozens of varieties on the table, and this is my take on the latter— with Duke's, of course. The secret to this pie is the crust: The toasted nuts and mayonnaise are a great contrast to the sweet coconut milk and toasted coconut filling. If you're in a hurry, you can top the coconut custard with sweetened whipped cream instead of meringue, but I think it's well worth the extra effort. Plus, you've already got egg whites left over from the filling so you might as well whip them up. Don't be intimidated by Italian meringue— it just takes patience and a good candy thermometer.

Recipe Continues

	Macadamia Nut Crust (recipe follows)
1	(13.5-ounce) can coconut milk
1½	cups half-and-half
5	large egg yolks
¾	cup sugar
¼	cup cornstarch
1	tablespoon salted butter
1	teaspoon vanilla extract
1½	cups sweetened flaked coconut, toasted
	Italian Meringue Topping (recipe follows)

1. Make the Macadamia Nut Crust.

2. Bring the coconut milk and half-and-half to a simmer in a medium saucepan.

3. Meanwhile, whisk together the egg yolks, sugar, and cornstarch in a medium bowl until pale and thickened. Gradually add about one-fourth of the hot milk mixture, whisking constantly. Whisk in the remaining milk and return the entire mixture to the saucepan.

4. Cook over medium-low heat, whisking constantly, until the mixture thickens (do not boil). Stir in the butter, vanilla, and coconut. Pour into the crust. Cover with plastic wrap and chill until cooled.

5. While the tart cools, make the Italian Meringue Topping.

6. Remove the tart from the refrigerator and top with the Italian Meringue Topping. Use a kitchen torch to toast the peaks, or place under a broiler for 30 to 60 seconds to toast.

Recipe Continues

MACADAMIA NUT
Crust

Makes 1 (10-inch) tart shell

1½ CUPS ALL-PURPOSE FLOUR

1 CUP CHOPPED MACADAMIA NUTS, TOASTED

¼ CUP GRANULATED SUGAR

½ CUP DUKE'S MAYONNAISE

1. Pulse the flour, nuts, and sugar in a food processor until crumbly. Add the mayonnaise and pulse until the mixture forms a dough. Pat the dough onto the bottom and up the sides of a 10-inch tart pan with removable bottom. Chill for 30 minutes.

2. Preheat the oven to 375°F. Bake the crust for 20 to 25 minutes, until browned and cooked through. Remove to a wire rack to cool completely.

ITALIAN MERINGUE
Topping

Makes about 3½ cups

6 LARGE EGG WHITES, AT ROOM TEMPERATURE

½ TEASPOON CREAM OF TARTAR

PINCH OF SALT

1 CUP GRANULATED SUGAR, DIVIDED

3 TABLESPOONS WATER

1. Beat the egg whites, cream of tartar, and salt in a heavy stand mixer at medium-high speed until soft peaks form. Gradually add ¼ cup of the sugar.

2. Meanwhile, bring the remaining ¾ cup sugar and the water to a boil in a small saucepan over medium heat, stirring to dissolve the sugar. (Brush down the sides of the pan with a wet pastry brush to dissolve any sugar crystals.) Boil, without stirring, for about 4 minutes, or until the mixture reaches 240°F (soft-ball stage) on a candy thermometer.

3. With the mixer running at medium speed, slowly pour the hot sugar mixture along the sides of the bowl into the egg white mixture. Increase the speed to high and beat for about 3 minutes, until the bowl is no longer hot and the mixture is glossy and firm.

Acknowledgments

As a freelancer mom, I am often asked, "How do you do it all?" And the truth is I don't—or at least not by myself. I have an amazing "village" that helped make this dream project a reality. I certainly couldn't have done it alone and have so many incredible people in my life to thank for it.

To my agent, Martha Hopkins: Thank you for believing in me—a girl who had the chops and experience to write her own book but no "platform." You went above and beyond to make this project happen—from helping perfect the book proposal to testing recipes. I am so lucky to call you not only my agent, but also my friend.

To my editor, Morgan Hedden: Thank you for loving the book proposal just the way it was. You've been wonderful to work with, encouraging me along the way, and I couldn't have asked for a better steward to see this project through to the end.

To everyone at Grand Central Publishing: Thank you for the opportunity to work together to create my dream cookbook. You all have been wonderful to collaborate with, and I hope we can bring each other success in the years to come.

To Erin Hatcher, director of marketing at Sauer Brands, Inc., and Caroline Creasey, assistant brand manager at Sauer Brands, Inc.: Thank you for trusting me with the Duke's brand. It was a joy creating recipes using my "secret ingredient," and I hope this book extends the Duke's fan base far and wide.

To my creative team, photographer Mary Britton Senseney, prop stylist Elizabeth Demos, and culinary assistant Bert John: You guys are the best and have been with me since the beginning. I know I've "arrived" when work doesn't feel like work. Thank you for inspiring me, for making such beautiful photos, for eating more mayo recipes than you would've liked, and for encouraging me all along the way.

To my designer, Laura Palese: Your inherent talent is evident in every book you design, and I am so fortunate to have had you work on this project. Somehow you were able to take what I was envisioning in my head and put it on paper, creating a design that was even more spectacular than I could have ever imagined. Thank you.

To my illustrator, Emily Wallace: Thank you for creating the perfect illustrations for this book. I'm so appreciative to have had you share your incredible talent.

To my beautifying gurus, Mitchell Hall and Genevieve Routon: Thank you for making me feel gorgeous during our shoot. The photos turned out better than I could ever have hoped for.

To my recipe testers: There are too many of you to list, but you know who you are. Thank you for taking time to test recipes for me.

To the contributing chefs and authors: Thank you for sharing your passion for Duke's with fans everywhere!

To all the mentors I've had along the way, including Nathalie Dupree: Thank you for your support over the years, for teaching me how to write a recipe, to be an editor, and to know when an idea you have is a good one. I've been blessed with an amazing group of lady bosses to teach me the ins and outs of the publishing world, and I owe a lot of my success to your advice and guidance.

To my parents: I wouldn't be where I am today if it weren't for you. From putting me through college and culinary school, to guiding me along the way and urging me to follow my passion. Thank you.

To my grandparents, both on earth and in heaven: Thank you for teaching me the love language of food. From sad pound cakes and pineapple sandwiches, to Mema dip, deviled crab, an RC Cola and a Moon Pie, these have been some of my favorite food memories.

To Anne, the world's best mother-in-law: Whether keeping Anderson entertained, driving around Charleston looking for ingredients for me, or tasting umpteen different recipes, thank you for all your help with day-to-day life while I was writing the book.

To Anderson: You are the inspiration for everything I do. I hope that my work on this cookbook encourages you to always follow your dreams.

And to save the best for last, to my husband, Chris: What a crazy ride it's been. This project couldn't have happened without your support. Thank you for always being my number one fan—even after washing countless sinks full of dirty dishes from recipe testing. I am the luckiest girl in the world to have you by my side. I couldn't have asked for a better travel partner, life partner, and friend.

Index

Ashley Strickland Freeman

is an award-winning food stylist, recipe developer, author, and editor based in Charleston, South Carolina. She received a degree in journalism from the University of Georgia and a degree in culinary arts from the French Culinary Institute (now The International Culinary Center). Ashley has written and contributed content for more than 45 cookbooks and other publications such as *Southern Living, Cooking Light, Weight Watchers, Betty Crocker*, and *Pillsbury* as well as for major brands like Lodge Cast Iron, Mars, Wonder Bread, and more, and she most recently was the food stylist for *Delicious Miss Brown* on the Food Network. Besides editing, developing, and testing recipes, she loves being a mom to son Anderson and traveling with her husband. This is her third cookbook. You can find her on Instagram at @ashleystricklandfreeman.